Short-Timer

Short-Timer

By

RICHARD A. HENRY

ARPress
ILLUMINATING IDEAS.
EMPOWERING VOICES

ARPress
45 Dan Road Suite 5
Canton MA 02021

Hotline: 1(888) 821-0229
Fax: 1(508) 545-7580

Ordering Information:

Quantity sales. Special discounts are available on quantity purchases by corporations, associations, and others. For details, contact the publisher at the address above.

Printed in the United States of America.

ISBN-13:		
	Paperback	979-8-89330-256-1
	eBook	979-8-89330-255-4
	Hardcover	979-8-89330-257-8

Library of Congress Control Number: 2024901494

TABLE OF CONTENTS

DEDICATION

In memory of my father, Junius S. Henry, U.S. Army World War II and Fletcher J. Nowlin, Jr., Killed in Action in Vietnam, during the battle for Hamburger Hill.

This book is also dedicated to all the children, men and women who got caught up in the war for control of Vietnam. May the memory of those who died there serve as a constant reminder that there are no winners in war. May those who survived stand vigil, and do all in their power to see to it that America never gets involved in another "Vietnam."

Last, but not least, this book is dedicated to my mother, Nancy E. Mitchell, who had sons serving in combat four and a half of the seven years that U.S. ground forces were officially involved in Vietnam.

A special thanks to, Biff for hanging in there.

INTRODUCTION

Where do you begin a story that began long before it actually happened? The bit of history I am about to tell is a mixture of perceived reality, wished-for reality and politically created reality.

It began with the Gulf of Tonkin incident; the now infamous event which happened and did not happen. The Gulf of Tonkin incident ended our unofficial involvement and marked the beginning of our official entry into what was alleged to be an official war between the unofficial-official government of The Republic of South Vietnam and the official-unofficial government of North Vietnam.

This is but a small part of the history of the War in Vietnam; America's longest war, where soldiers of all ethnic backgrounds and colors fought side by side. It was a war being fought halfway around the world while at home a war against racism and injustice raged. It was a war where flashing the peace sign was perfectly acceptable while waving a clinched fist in the air, the black power symbol, was a court martial offense. It was a war where back at base camps, whites openly called blacks "nigger," and blacks angrily cursed "honkies." Vietnam was a war where racism reared its ugly head on far too many an occasion, and in many different ways.

The final statistics tell part of the tale. Blacks suffered a death rate that was almost four times greater than their percentage of the American population. Black Marines whose military occupations were cooks, drivers, supply personnel, etc., were routinely assigned to infantry combat duty. While on the other hand, white Marines who were 0311's (Infantry Rifleman), or plainly stated, highly trained combatants, were routinely given choice jobs in the rear which greatly increased their chances of returning to the real world. Yet, when it counted most, in the heat of combat, there were no niggers, spics, wetbacks or honkies; just young American men barely past puberty, fighting and dying together while hoping to survive the nightmare of war.

Death is colorblind. Oftentimes the tears flowed freely and the pain was felt by all without regard for race, color or creed as men mourned and comforted each other over the death of a fallen comrade.

This story is without specific dates. To those of us who served our country in Vietnam, they are not that important. For us, Vietnam remains a vast period of time in our not-so-distant past, which still lives with us today and will be with us tomorrow. It is the story of the brave young American men of every hue who spent a "lifetime" in Vietnam.

This is not a political novel, nor is it an attempt to pass judgment on the issue of whether America's military involvement in Vietnam was justified or not. If questions about the moral ethics of war entered the minds of those of us who served our country in Vietnam, it did so either before we arrived "in country" or after we returned to the "real world." Surviving the horror that was Vietnam called for concentrating on making it from one moment to the next.

This story is dedicated to the Vietnam combat veteran. Filled with the pain, fear, suffering and the general discomforts experienced by the average fighting man in Vietnam, it also depicts the warmth, humor, and friendship that was necessary for survival in a crazy war that never should have been and never can be forgotten by millions.

CHAPTER ONE

It was anything but a dull trip. The train began its journey from New York, headed for South Carolina. It was a special train, filled with young men on their way to Army basic training in North Carolina or Marine Corps boot camp in South Carolina. The group of youthful men consisted of a mixture of blacks, whites, and a sprinkling of Hispanics. The proportion of blacks was far greater than the ratio of blacks to whites in the general American population. The stops made along the way could explain that in part. The first out of New York was Newark, followed by stops in Camden, Philadelphia, Baltimore, Washington, D.C., Richmond, and a final one, to pick up additional "passengers," in Norfolk, Virginia.

First, I wondered why there were civil law enforcement officers along with military authorities at several stops. After engaging in conversation with a few of the "passengers," I quickly found out. It seemed the recruits ranged from those who had volunteered for military service out of a desire to serve, to those who were drafted into service, and lastly, to those who had volunteered to serve their country in the military as an alternative to serving time in prison.

There was an abundance of interesting stories told along the way. The guys who had been solicited into the service of

1

America to help stamp out Communism in South Vietnam, as opposed to stamping out license plates in prison somewhere in retribution for a wide variety of crimes, had the liveliest to tell. Although the tales differed, the storytellers all seemed to have one thing in common; the belief that they had beaten the system by agreeing to join the service instead of going to prison. Maybe some had, but for many, it wouldn't work out that way. Their decision would cost them their lives.

Most of us were still youngsters, just out of high school or fresh from the streets, where we delighted in playing semi-grown-up versions of childhood games. It didn't matter where we came from, or our present maturity level, because the reality of being an adult would soon hit us.

Almost six hours after departing New York, the train stopped in Washington, D.C., where another group of new recruits and draftees were ushered aboard. A few minutes later, we were rolling smoothly along the tracks to Richmond when a fight broke out between several white recruits. I have searched my memory, and I still can't recall how it started. It just happened.

Within minutes, and for no apparent good reason, what started as a simple fight between two individuals, turned into a massive brawl between those of us destined to become Marines and those who were on their way to become soldiers. It was one hell of a riot, and our first experience at what hand to hand combat would be like. Weapons of all sorts seemed to appear out of nowhere. In what seemed like forever, a lot of blood was spilled, and many bones broken. The conductor must have radioed ahead to Richmond, because when the train pulled into the station, around twenty minutes after the fight broke out, dozens of military police boarded swinging their highly-polished, black nightsticks, and quickly put an end to the trouble. After taking the seriously injured off the train and tending to the lesser wounded, the MP's separated the Marine recruits from the Army recruits. A contingent of MP's remained aboard until after the Army recruits departed the train in North Carolina.

The remainder of the train ride to South Carolina was uneventful. Some Marine recruits napped. A few could be heard talking about what they imagined boot camp would be like. Still, others talked about how they couldn't wait to get to Vietnam and kill some gooks. There was one recruit sitting directly behind me who kept staring at a picture in his hand stopping occasionally to wipe a tear from his eye. I got up and sat in the seat next to him to see what was wrong and comfort him if I could. He was holding a photo of his brother dressed in combat gear, holding an M-14 rifle. He explained that the picture had been taken six months earlier, in Vietnam, and that his brother had been killed two months after the picture was snapped.

He wasn't crying because he was scared. It seemed important to him that I understood it was because he was angry with those slant-eyed, communist bastards who had killed his brother, and he couldn't wait to pay them back. I had not had training in psychology, but knew enough to know that the guy had gone to lunch one day and never came back. With that in mind, I slowly got up and returned to my seat. The brother next to me asked me what was this guy's problem? I told him the story as told to me. We just looked at each other and frowned as though to say, "He's gone already."

I had made friends with the recruit seated next to me back at Fort Hamilton in Brooklyn, New York. His last name was Jones. It's funny how quickly one can become conditioned to a new way of thinking. We were sworn into the military for less than a day and already we were introducing ourselves and addressing one another by our last names.

Jones was born and raised in Harlem, a few blocks from the St. Nicholas Housing Projects where I grew up. He was among the group on board the train who was given the choice of either going to jail or to Parris Island. He chose Parris Island, South Carolina as the lesser of the two evils. He made it quite clear to me that he had no intention of finishing boot camp, much less ever going to Vietnam.

We were sitting in silence a few minutes, when suddenly Jones began to chuckle. I turned to him and asked, "What's so funny?" His chuckle turned to a loud laugh. After a few moments of side-splitting laughter, he regained his composure long enough to tell me.

"I was just thinking of that clown back at Fort Hamilton who tried to fake being deaf. Did you see that fool?"

"I sure did."

The incident that Jones had just reminded me of was pretty funny. Shortly after we arrived for our initial physical at Fort Hamilton they administered a hearing test to all the potential new members of the armed forces. This guy, named Furman, who up until that point hadn't shown any problem with his hearing, suddenly turned to me.

"Check this out," he said.

"Check what out?" I inquired. Before he could answer, a big, burly looking, bass-voiced sergeant called his name, and directed him to be seated for his hearing test. Furman took a seat next to the testing machine and placed the headphones over his ears, as instructed.

It was at that point that I realized what he had wanted me to check out. I mean, the guy was really good! He acted as though he couldn't hear a sound. He sat staring blankly while the tester continually turned up the sound. I was standing a full six feet away from Furman and the machine and could not help but grit my teeth from the sound that I imagined by now was loud enough to burst the average person's eardrums. Furman didn't flinch an inch during the entire test.

After a few minutes, the tester yanked the headphones off Furman's head, told him he had a hearing problem, and the service had no use for someone who was almost deaf. The sergeant then shouted at him to go and take a seat in the rear of the room. Furman headed to the back, turned toward Jones and me and gave us a quick wink as though to say, "so long guys."

The battery of physical tests continued for the rest of us while Furman sat off to the side flipping through a magazine he had brought to the induction center. Around an hour after Furman failed his hearing test, a corporal carrying two large metal buckets sneaked up behind him. The corporal stopped just inches from the back of Furman's chair and, with a pail held firmly in each arm, raised his arms high above his head. He stood there a second or two, then suddenly released his hold. The buckets crashed to the tile floor, making a loud clanging sound. Everyone in the room, who hadn't seen what the corporal was up to, was startled, except Furman. He didn't flinch at all.

"Man is he good," I commented to Jones.

Several hours passed. It was somewhere around noon when a sergeant announced that we would take a break from our physicals for lunch. I followed the sergeant with the rest of the men facing military service. On the way out of the room, I glanced over at Furman. He appeared to be napping. Another corporal seated at a desk, which was at least fifteen feet from where Furman was seated, announced in a lower-than-normal voice, "Mr. Furman you can go home now."

Without hesitating a second and obviously without thinking, Furman sprung to his feet. "Thank you!" Furman responded and took a step towards the door before he stopped dead in his tracks. He realized that he had just made a major blunder. Two MPs walked over and escorted him into another room. We didn't see him after that.

After recalling the incident, I joined Jones in laughter. We continued to laugh as we reminded each other of another of the day's more humorous events. Back at the induction center there was the big husky guy from Flatbush who looked like he ate steel for breakfast. When he stripped down at the start of the physical, he was dressed in a pair of red, women's bikini underwear, with matching bra. Once the recruit stepped clear of his pants, he lifted the doctor standing in front of him off his feet, planted a whopping kiss on his lips, put the doctor back on the floor and spoke in a high pitched voice. "I can't wait to join the Army and get my hands on all those gorgeous young men."

Everyone in line broke out in a riotous laughter. We laughed so hard that the jock, who had obviously undergone much painstaking planning on his scheme to get out of military service, couldn't restrain his own. Needless to say, he finished the physical with flying colors.

Jones and I spent the next half-hour recalling a few other funny incidents that had taken place that day. We were chuckling almost continuously, until we noticed a guy hobbling down the aisle of the railroad car. We looked at one another, turned back to the guy, then eyed each other again. We were momentarily confused. Obviously, someone had made a mistake. "How in the hell did he pass the physical?" I asked my newfound friend. Jones just looked at me in utter disbelief and shrugged his shoulders. We figured that maybe the guy didn't belong on the train.

That's it, I thought, and turned to Jones. "I have to ask him if he's going where we're headed, or somehow got on the wrong train."

"No you're not," Jones replied, challenging me to do so.

I didn't need to be dared because I already had every intention of asking. I climbed over Jones' out-stretched legs and walked to where the subject of our conversation had taken a seat.

"Excuse me," I said, as I sat down on the arm of his chair. "Yes?" he asked somewhat nervously.

"I'm not trying to be funny or anything, but are you headed for Parris Island?"

"Sure am!" he replied proudly, without hesitation. "What happened to your leg?" I asked boldly.

"My uncle accidentally shot me on a hunting trip back home, when I was ten. They had to remove a part of my bone, but I've been okay since then."

"Where are you from?"

"Home is in West Virginia. My daddy upped and brung us to Richmond when the mine closed down back home, a few years ago."

He proceeded to tell me about what he had been doing for the past few years. I couldn't resist asking him how he wound up on a train heading for Marine Corps Boot Camp.

"I was walking past this recruiting station a few weeks ago, when this Marine sergeant stopped me and asked, 'How would you like to become a Marine, son?' I told him I would love to, only I had a bum leg. He told me the Marine Corps worked miracles. He said they would fit me with a pair of special boots while I was in boot camp and afterwards, they would operate on my leg and fix it back to normal. So here I am."

Well, you can imagine the look of complete and absolute dismay on my face as I listened to his story. My mouth was hanging wide open. Holy shit! I don't believe it, I thought to myself.

The thought that this guy might be representative of the typical mentality of someone I might have to depend on to save my life one day, momentarily frightened me. Between him and the bunch of should-have-been jailbirds riding the train, I knew that boot camp would be a hell of an experience. I politely excused myself and returned to my seat, still wearing my shocked expression.

"What's wrong with you?" Jones asked.

I proceeded to tell him about the conversation I just had, and the look on Jones' face began to resemble what I imagined my face must have looked like as I listened to the guy's story just moments earlier.

"And you think I'm going to stick with this shit," Jones mumbled aloud to himself, as he turned and looked in the direction of the handicapped recruit from Richmond.

After exchanging a few comments about the obviously not- so-wrapped-too-tight recruit from Virginia, Jones and I talked about how desperate recruiters must be to make their quotas. It wasn't long before we struck up a conversation about what it was like growing up in Harlem.

We quickly discovered that we had grown up only a few blocks apart, but couldn't recall having ever seen one another before. That wasn't unusual for people living in a large city. Hell, you could grow up in a city as large as New York and not even know all the people living in the same building as you.

Jones was three years older than I and, as it turned out, knew my older brother. This seemed to solidify our newfound friendship. He was surprised to find out that my brother had been in the Marines for more than three years and had done eighteen months in Vietnam.

We continued to recall how it was to be young and living in Harlem during the late fifties and early sixties. Although he had attended public school and I a parochial school, we were able to talk with the greatest of ease. We soon found that outside the school setting we had experienced many of the same things. We hung out in the same parks and we both recalled the challenge of riding down Deadman's Hill on a fix (a ten speed bike without brakes).

Deadman's Hill was the name we gave to a steep incline located on 127th Street. It started at the top in St. Nicholas Park and ended at the bottom, on St. Nicholas Avenue. The trick was being able to stop the fix once you reached the bottom. If you didn't stop in time, you could wind up splattered all over St. Nicholas Avenue. Riding down the hill was just one of those things you did to show your buddies you weren't chicken. We laughed as we agreed that anyone who said they weren't scared as hell the first time they rode down Deadman's Hill was lying.

We remembered several other fun things we did while growing up in Harlem. We talked about the finer points of stoopball and the best way to shoot a loadies top. You needed a loadies top to play skellies. A loadies top was a bottle cap filled with clay or mud.

Skellies was a game in which you had to get down on the ground on your hands and knees to play. The game board was a large square drawn on the pavement with chalk. Inside the large square, you drew smaller boxes, one box in each corner and four sets of double boxes between the corner boxes. You then numbered them one through twelve, alternating between the far corners and the boxes opposite each other.In the center of the main box, you drew a small box surrounded by a larger box that was sectioned into four parts. Each section contained a letter. One contained the letter I, another the letter A, the third section the letter K, and the fourth section contained the letter D. Together they stood for I Am Killer Diller.

The object of the game was to pluck or shoot your loadies top around the boxes with your fingers, until you entered the center box. You then worked your way around the sections marked I, A, K, D. After entering the center box marked thirteen, you had to work your way back down to the first box. When you reached the first box again, the game was over for you. Everyone else who had been playing continued until there was only one person left, and even he had to finish before he could stop playing. If you quit, you were banished for a long time before you were invited to join in another game of skellies.

You could work your way up and down the boxes in one of two ways. You could either pluck your top into the correct box or you could carefully take aim and shoot at someone else's top. If you hit it, you advanced to the next box and so on. We paused a moment as I commented to Jones that in many ways skellies could be compared to what we were about to go through. We would work our way through thirteen weeks of boot camp to become killer dillers, and soon afterward, would be shipped off to Vietnam. Once there, we would have to make it through thirteen months, instead of thirteen boxes, before we could call it a day and go home. Before I could say anything else, Jones interrupted. "That's what you are about to go through, not me. I keep telling you, I'm getting out."

We chatted a while longer. I tried in vain to pry the details from Jones of how he planned to get out of the Marines without getting a dishonorable discharge. He just smiled, repeated that he was getting out and wouldn't get a dishonorable discharge in the process. Then he closed his eyes, and in a few minutes, he was fast asleep and still smiling broadly. I looked at my watch.

It was 3:30 in the morning. We would be arriving soon. From what I remembered my brother telling me, I would need my rest. I pressed the button on the arm of the seat and it slid back, as I nestled comfortably against it. What will Marine Corps boot camp be like? I wondered before drifting to sleep.

CHAPTER TWO

The bright sunrays shining through the train window awakened me. I rubbed the sleep from my eyes and glanced at my watch. It was a few minutes past six A.M., and although I'd only had a couple of hours of sleep, I felt rested and alert. We should be arriving at our destination in less than half an hour, I thought, as I stared out the window at the sunrise. It was the most beautiful one that I had seen in a long time. Coming of age in New York City rarely presents the opportunity to see firsthand how spectacular a sunrise could be. The sun appeared to be growing by leaps and bounds as it rose, ever so gently, over the distant hilltops.

The awesome sight of a new day arriving so majestically had me nearly mesmerized, when suddenly without warning, my stomach tightened. I was beginning to get that feeling that nearly everyone experiences at one time or another, the emotion that overcomes you when you are ready to step into a new phase of life. The feelings you get on your first day of high school and again on graduation day; that sort of tingling sensation you get when you move out of your parents' home into your first apartment; the feeling you get when you report for your first day on a new job.

I studied the sunrise for the next fifteen minutes. The huge, fiery, orange ball seemed to be perched atop the mountain in the distance, its piercing rays delivering a message to the recruits, who had begun to awaken. It appeared to be telling us that we were about to experience a new phase in our lives.

Jones was one of the last recruits to awaken. He looked over at me, wiped the sleep from his eyes and asked, "What time is it?"

"Six-twenty."

"What time are we supposed to get there?"

"We should be pulling into the station in ten minutes or so." "Then what?"

"How should I know. It's my first trip here, same as you." Jones and I exchanged nervous smiles.

Moments later, the conductor entered the car and announced, "Rise and shine everyone. We will be pulling into the station in less than ten minutes." Then he proceeded to the next car, where he could be heard repeating his announcement.

A mounting tension could be felt throughout the car as the recruits scrambled to get their personal belongings together. The train sluggishly rolled into the station and came to an abrupt stop alongside the platform. Everyone remained seated. Before anyone could volunteer to be the first off the train, three picture book Marines boarded. The last to climb aboard was a corporal, the largest of the three, and apparently the one with biggest mouth as well.

"Well what are you waiting for ladies? Get your piss asses off this train. Your butts belong to the Marine Corps now. Move it!"

We filed off and stood along the platform until the three Marines who had ordered us off the train exited. A convoy of buses slowly rolled to where we stood. Again, the corporal shouted. "Everyone listen up. When the buses stop and the doors open, I want your asses on them and seated ASAP." The response was an immediate dead silence. Jones looked at me and smirked. "My ass will be on a bus out of here ASAP."

Immediately after the buses stopped, their doors swung open and the three Marines, as though they had suddenly lost their collective minds, began running among us shouting, "Move it! Move it! We ain't got all day. You're on Marine Corps' time now. Hustle your butts, maggots."

Mumblings of, "Oh shit!" and other choice words could be heard from the recruits as we scrambled aboard the buses that seemed to be waiting to devour our entire lives up to that exact point in time. Once the last recruit boarded the bus, the three Marines, who had so graciously greeted our arrival, strutted to a jeep parked by the side of the station house and climbed in. I pressed my face against the bus window and could see the three of them as they laughed and slapped one another on the hand. Less than a minute later, the jeep pulled in front of the lead bus, signaling the driver to close the doors. Two minutes later, we were on our way. Next stop, Parris Island.

"What do you think boot camp will be like?" I asked Jones.

"I haven't the slightest idea, nor do I care. I won't be there long enough to find out," he reminded me.

For the first time, I began to grow a little apprehensive about what lay ahead. Numerous thoughts flowed freely and uncontrollably throughout my mind. Did I have what it took to get through Marine Corps boot camp? Did I really even care? Those were but two of my self-imposed questions.

After about fifteen minutes or so of succumbing to minor paranoia, I regained control of my mind. I decided that a refreshing piece of Bazooka bubble gum was needed to calm my nerves. As I dug through my small gym bag searching for it, I suddenly noticed that everyone had stopped talking. It wasn't necessary to look up to know we had arrived at our final destination. Slowly, I raised my head and glanced out the window in time to see the huge sign that read; MARINE CORPS RECRUIT DEPOT PARRIS ISLAND, SOUTH CAROLINA.

In less than ten minutes, the buses rolled to a stop in front of the Recruit Receiving Barracks. Immaculately clean grounds and drill fields could be seen everywhere you looked.

"This is it," I said to Jones, who was shaking his head from side to side in apparent disbelief at what he saw.

"This is shit!" he responded.

Before we could exchange further words, the bus door swung open, and a drill instructor popped his head inside and began shouting.

"Well, what are you ladies waiting for. Get a move on. This ain't no Sunday picnic."

We filed off the bus, assisted by the continuous bellowing of several drill instructors. I whispered to Jones.

"I guess the main requirement for becoming a DI is a big mouth."

Jones started to crack a smile, but was cut off from completing it by the growling of the DI standing at the foot of the steps.

"Wipe that shit-eating grin off your face maggot," he yelled directly at Jones, then quickly jerked his head in my

15

direction. "Lock those jaws, sissy. From now on, you'll speak only when spoken to. That goes for everyone," he added in a deafening voice, which seemed to echo. "Move your asses. Line up in a straight line on the white lines in front of you. Keep your mouths shut and your eyes glued straight ahead." Our response to his commands was immediate. We reacted as participants in a well-rehearsed play.

A few minutes later, we were ushered, so to speak, into a massive open room where we were instructed to fall in along more rows of white lines and stand at arms' length from each other. We stood there while several drill instructors strolled in and out of our ranks looking us up and down and making a battery of not so flattering remarks.

"Will you look at this load of shit," one remarked. "A bunch of city fairies," shouted another.

"Keep your eyes straight before I knock them clear to the rear of your box head," a DI shrieked at a nervous and frightened recruit. The DI stood in front of him, almost touching the recruit's nose with his own as he continued to shout insults.

Most of the black recruits were lined up next to each other. Two of the drill instructors approached us, then came to an abrupt halt. The taller of the two slowly rotated his head from left to right then back, looked at us, then tilted his head toward the ceiling lights and down again. He turned to his counterpart. "Well, lookie here, lookie here, an unscheduled eclipse. Break this dark spot up," he shouted. He immediately followed his order with specific instructions to the black recruits to disperse and mix in with the others.

After the "dark spot" dissipated, the DIs continued to move up and down the formation while singling out several

16

recruits for individualized harassment. This continued for some twenty odd minutes before we were sectioned into groups of seventy- five and, for lack of a better way to put it, introduced to our drill instructors. I knew right then and there that training was to be anything but a picnic. When one of your DIs was named Staff Sergeant Sargen, you knew that you were in for a hell of a time. Jones and I were assigned to Recruit Training Platoon 2057.

The DIs spent the next half-hour laying down the law of the Marine Corps as they saw it and trying to instill the fear of God in us, as manifested through them. Our Senior Drill Instructor, SSgt. Jarrell, gave a sermon that could have won him "Preacher of the Year Award" at an annual Southern Baptist convention. It seemed that we had committed the gravest of all sins. We had been born civilians.

"Look at you. Civilian scum balls. Pieces of whale shit. You look like civilians and, worst yet, you smell like civilians. When I'm done with you, those of you who make it will thank me because you'll be United States Marines. Until then, you're lower than whale shit. And that's at the bottom of the ocean," he shouted.

Just as SSgt. Jerrall was finishing his first of many sermons, one recruit made the unforgivable mistake of swatting a bug resting on his cheek. All four drill instructors present seemed to have a sudden attack of lunacy. They rushed over and surrounded the now petrified recruit and began screaming at him. SSgt. Sargen shouted in his left ear, Sgt. Lundquist in his right. SSgt. Jerrall stood yelling directly in front of him and Sgt. Copeland was to his rear. Their lips moved in perfect synchronization, ringing out in harmony. "You just killed one of my sand flies. Don't you ever kill another Marine

Corps sand fly as long as you live. Do you understand me, maggot?"

The recruit, who by now looked like he was ready to shit in his pants if he hadn't already done so, answered in a somewhat cracked voice, "Yes, sir."

"I can't hear you!" shouted all four drill instructors, again sounding like a professional acappella group.

The recruit responded immediately, crying out, "Yes, sir," with such force that I thought the veins which had appeared across the top of his now reddened forehead would burst. SSgt. Jarrell quickly stepped out from between the line of recruits and began bellowing. "When I ask one of you ladies a question, I want to hear all you answer, 'Yes, sir,' loud and clear. Do I make myself clear?" We responded without a moment's hesitation.

"Yes, sir!"

"I can't hear you."

"Yes, sir!" we hollered again, straining our untrained civilian voices.

"That's better ladies," he replied.

Next, we were issued some quick instructions on how to march, then herded off to our barracks. It was a riot to observe seventy-five recruits trying to march together for the first time. A few guys stumbled over their own feet. Others tried to keep in step with the recruit immediately in front of them. Some ran in an effort to keep up with the group. We hurried along, aided by our drill instructors, who ran back and forth screaming their heads off.

No sooner had we arrived at the barracks that was to be our home for the next several months, than we were rushed back out to stand in neat lines again. Later, I was to learn that the Marine Corps was quite fond of hurrying you up, only to have you waiting in or on a line. Because of that little practice, to this day, I can't stand waiting in line.

Things continued to move rapidly the remainder of the day. Our first stop after leaving the barracks was a large hall, where we each had a number scribbled across our chest. This was supposed to help with processing and equipment issue. Next stop was the barbershop and goodbye hair. A short while later, we were waiting in line again to pick up our initial issue of clothing which consisted of a utility coat, two pairs of trousers, two blouses (shirts), two caps, skivvies (a strange name for underwear), socks and boots.

While I waited for everyone else to finish, I amused myself by reading the labels inside the clothing. It seemed to me that a frustrated writer, fired from a Madison Avenue advertising agency in New York City, wrote all the labels for military clothing. A typical label read: COAT, MAN'S FIELD WITH HOOD, NYLON COTTON SATTEEN OG-107, DSA 100-69-C- 0760 SMALL REGULAR CHEST: FROM 33 to 37 inches HEIGHT: FROM 67 TO 71 inches STOCK NO. 8405-782-2936.

It amazed me that it took all that just to identify a jacket.

Next on the agenda was a complete physical, Marine Corps style. We were X-rayed everywhere imaginable. The worse part of the examination was the inoculations. The medics appeared to take great pleasure in inflicting as much suffering as possible while they shot holes in you with their shining needle guns.

Bucket and rifle issue followed our physicals. The bucket was full of what at the time seemed to be the weirdest assortment of buckles, poles, straps and other items. Collectively, they were called 782 gear. To this day, I haven't the slightest idea how they came up with that title.

In addition to the items listed above, 782 gear consisted of a canteen, cup, haversack, knapsack, half of a tent, tent poles, tent pegs and a variety of sundry items. Included in our gear was a housewife. That was the name given to a sewing kit.

Not long after we were issued some of our basic gear, I experienced my first taste of Marine Corps chow. It took some getting used to. I only wish then that I had seen a reference to Marine Corps chow that I ran across a few months after I finished boot camp. It would have helped me to fool myself into thinking I was eating "Good, delicious, hot food, tops in energy and vitamin content. Food prepared by experts," as advertised in the pamphlet.

The bulk of the remainder of the day was spent standing in and on one line after another. I had no idea what time it was when we finally returned to the barracks. What does linger in my memory is the feeling of complete exhaustion I experienced that first day. Something else I'll never forget is an incident that resulted in my being the first in my platoon to demonstrate jumping jacks.

We were standing in front of our bunks, moments away from finally being able to climb into them for some much-needed sleep, when the guy next to me began to cry. SSgt. Sargen rushed over and stood in front of him. "What the hell's wrong with you faggot?" he inquired sarcastically.

Well, you could imagine the looks on the rest of our faces when, without shame, the recruit (or boot as we were called) blurted out, "I miss my mommy."

By now, several of us were summoning up every ounce of will power we could to keep from bursting out laughing which was a definite no-no at such an early stage in training. I was able to contain mine, until the end of the following exchange between our DI and the recruit.

"How old are you son?" SSgt. Sargen asked.

"Seventeen, sir," the weeping recruit answered rather sheepishly.

"Well, you better get this through your head right now. Your mommy doesn't miss you none. No boy, she don't miss you for a second. She signed your ass in here, didn't she?"

At that point, the recruit began to really wail. I think I saved him from the wrath of our seasoned DI because I could no longer contain myself and almost buckled over laughing. Mind you, I wasn't the only one. I just had the misfortune of being the closest to SSgt. Sargen who immediately turned his unwanted attention to me. "You like to laugh, do you worm?"

"No, sir!" I shouted while trying to erase the wrinkles from my cheeks. He gave me a stern look before he turned away and shouted, "Lights out!"

Everyone immediately proceeded to climb into their bunks. My forward motion was abruptly ended by a firm grasp on my arm. "Not you, smiley. You come with me."

I turned and followed SSgt. Sargen into the hallway, where he instructed me to start doing jumping jacks and to keep jumping and counting out loud until he returned and told me to stop.

Finally, after what seemed like an eternity, but in reality, was no more than thirty minutes, SSgt. Sargen returned and told me to go get in my bunk and go to sleep. I needn't tell you what a welcome relief sleep was that night.

CHAPTER THREE

If you were in relatively good physical condition when you arrived at boot camp, the physical training and long hours didn't seem to bother you much after the first two weeks. Such was the case for me. When I started boot camp, I was a couple of months shy of my nineteenth birthday, six feet-two and weighed one hundred and fifty pounds. I had never been a drinker and I didn't smoke. Although a child of the sixties, I hadn't experience with any type of drugs, not even marijuana. Running had been a hobby of mine, so by the end of the second week at Parris Island the early morning three mile runs that had become a part of our daily routine, were a breeze for me. For others, it was quite painful.

By then, a little reshuffling had taken place within the various training platoons. All the fat-bodies, a name given to those who were overweight and couldn't keep up with the rest of us, were transferred to the fat-body platoon. There they were exercised and placed on a strict diet until they slimmed down. A variety of methods were used to that end. One ritual they had to endure went like this: the DI's would march all the fat-bodies into the mess hall after everyone else had sat down to chow. Piles of food were dumped onto their trays. No sooner than they were seated and had taken in a mouthful or two of food, the fat-bodies had to get back up, empty their still full trays and exit the mess hall. Pure torture for them and funny to the rest of us, though we didn't dare exhibit our amusement.

Other recruits who didn't fit in had been transferred to CC platoon. The letters CC stood for "Crippled and Crazy." All the recruits who had a physical deformity, handicap or some recognizable mental deficiency were transferred there. It was a holding platoon where they passed away the time until they could be reprocessed out of the Marine Corps, which took several weeks. But these soon to be ex-recruits didn't sit around doing nothing all day. They were used to perform a wide variety of menial jobs.

I knew two of the guys in CC platoon. The recruit I met on the train with one leg shorter than the other and the second was recriut, soon to be civilian, Jones. He had somehow managed to convince everyone that he was not only illiterate, but also slightly off his rocker. On every written exam we took, during our first week at Parris Island, Jones simply sat there doodling all over the test papers. He also was quite adept at faking memory lapses and trances. It didn't take the Marine Corps very long to decide that they wanted no part of him.

Whenever we marched past CC platoon, Jones would throw me a wink. I often wonder how he made out in life. He was one of those people that you could sense would never bother anyone. The type of person who justs wanted to be left alone. There were recruits in CC platoon who were missing fingers, others were legally blind and some were legitimately out of their minds. How ninety-nine percent of them wound up at Parris Island in the first place puzzled me.

After we had been in boot camp for three weeks, we were told the "good news." It was announced that boot camp would be shortened from thirteen to eight weeks. The thought that something, in fact, a lot, was to be shaved from our training really worried me. It seemed to me that if you were preparing men for war, you would increase and not decrease their training.

The next few weeks were filled with countless hours of exercising, running, and attending a variety of classes. It didn't take long before even in my sleep, I could hear that all too familiar sound of HUP, TWO, THREEP, FO, YO, LEF.

One of the essential parts of boot camp was the two weeks spent on the rifle range. Before reporting to the range, we spent many hours learning what was called the Manual of Arms. This was a sequence of drills designed to teach us a series of positions and movements using the rifle. These movements looked mighty snappy when marching or as part of an inspection. It always struck me that if something was eliminated from boot camp training, it should have been the time spent mastering the Manual of Arms. I'm sure that if you asked any combat veteran if learning it had helped him use his rifle any better in Vietnam, you would probably get a negative frown instead of a verbal answer.

There were several other aspects of our tutelage that could have been eliminated and replaced with more useful training. We learned how important it was to take care of our rifles, including the proper way to clean and oil the wooden stock and butt of the M-14. "Take care of your rifle, and it would take care of you," we were told. That made sense at the time. Another "important" prerequisite to firing our rifles for the first time was that you had to be able to disassemble your

M-14 rifle in two minutes, and reassemble it in one while blind-folded.

You're probably thinking, if you're training men to be fighters, they should know everything that they can about their basic weapon, the rifle, right? Normally, I would agree with you. But, in actuality, we wasted much valuable time learning how to care for the M-14. However, I didn't find out what a waste it was until later when I arrived in Vietnam.

After learning everything there was to know about the standard issue weapon of the Marine Corps in boot camp, and later training with it in Infantry Training School, I had become a master of my M-14. We were required to memorize every word of the famous Marine Corps masterpiece of literary composition entitled "My Rifle." It is a gem. It read as follows:

This is my rifle. There are many like it, but this one is mine. My rifle is my best friend. I must master it as I master my life. My rifle, without me is useless. Without my rifle, I am useless. I must fire my rifle true. I must shoot straighter than my enemy, who is trying to kill me. I must shoot him before he shoots me. I will. My rifle and myself know that what counts in war is not the rounds we fire, the noise of our burst, nor the smoke we make. We know that it is the hits that count. We will hit.

My rifle is human, even as I, because it is my life. Thus, I will learn it as a brother. I will learn its weakness, its strength, its parts, its accessories, its sights and its barrel. I will keep my rifle clean and ready, even as I am clean and ready. We will become part of each other. We will. Before God I swear this creed. My rifle and myself are the defenders of my country. We are the masters of our enemy. We are the saviors of my life. So be it, until victory is America's and there is no enemy, but peace! Now I'll explain what I meant earlier when I said that much time was wasted learning all about the M-14; how to parade with it, how to stand inspection with it and how to keep its wooden parts from rotting. You see three and a half months after I finished all my training and arrived in Vietnam, I was issued an M-16 rifle instead of an M-14. Sometime between when I went on leave and when I arrived in Vietnam, the Marine Corps had taken the M-14 out of service and adopted the M-16 as the standard rifle. The M-16 was shorter and had a plastic stock and butt. It broke open like a shot gun for cleaning, instead of into five basic parts, as did the M-14. All the time spent learning how to care for, handle, disassemble and reassemble the M-14 was wasted. The bottom line was that, months later, when I arrived in Vietnam, I found myself dependent on a total stranger for my survival, instead of "my brother."

In boot camp, mail-call was probably the best part of the day. That is, if you got any. However, you were better off not receiving mail than having some young lady send you a perfumed letter. That meant pure hell. Yep, you paid in sweat for receiving a sweet-smelling letter.

By the end of my sixth week, I was well on my way to earning the hard-earned title of United States Marine. It took weeks, but finally I had learned there was a definite use for every item in my 782 gear. When it was my platoons' turn for mess duty, I avoided the drudgeries usually associated with it. I had become the favorite boot of several of my drill instructors.

When it came time for mess duty, I lucked out. My job was to act as a liaison between the mess sergeant and the other boots in my platoon. I simply went back and forth from the mess offices to the kitchen and dining area, relaying orders.

Actually, I got away with quite a few things in boot camp, one of which I owed to my inability to grow facial hair. At eighteen, my face was as smooth as a newborn baby's butt. Not even a hint of hair could be found on my face. Our DI's seemed to have an endless list of time-tested methods to motivate us. For example, whenever my platoon performed unsatisfactory as far as our DI's were concerned, they had a nifty way of inspiring us to do better next time. We had to line up in front of our bunks, take out our shaving gear, lather up and without benefit of a mirror, expected to be clean-shaven in all of sixty seconds.

When I say we, I actually mean them. Here was the catch: I wasn't required to lather up with my fellow boots (another name we were called), instead I served as a measuring device. Once the sixty seconds were up, our drill instructor would march down the aisle to inspect everyone's shave. As he inspected each boot, I had to walk alongside him. Our DI kept one hand on my cheek at all times. He would then rub his free hand along the shaven face of each of the other members of the platoon and make a comparison. If the shaved face didn't feel as smooth as mine, the recruit had to drop to the floor and pump off fifty push-ups. When I say my face was smooth, I mean it was smooth!

As expected, not many of my fellow recruits passed the inspection. Unfortunately, I'm sure I made some enemies because of it. I really did feel sorry for a few of them. Often, they would cut their face to shreds rushing to clear the lather off with the razor before the allotted time was up. If someone didn't finish shaving within the allotted time, there was an additional penalty of five hundred jumping jacks for that individual.

Another interesting part of boot camp was what was called "Free-Time." Usually, on Sunday, and occasionally during weekday evenings, there was time set aside for us to pursue the more "leisurely activities" of life. Ninety percent of our free time was spent washing clothes, starching covers (a strange term for a hat), cleaning gear and rifles, shining buckles and polishing boots. If there was enough time left, we could write a short letter or two. We were told that free time was designed to add to our living comfort, and to relieve the stress of our vigorous, training schedule.

An important aspect of our training was the time spent at the pool. I remember that day very clearly. We arrived around eight a.m. The swimming instructor was waiting and immediately greeted us.

"All right," he said.

"I want all of you who can swim to line up at the deep end of the pool. All non- swimmers and darkies, line up at the shallow end."

Being a fairly decent swimmer, I chose to act as though I hadn't heard his reference to darkies and joined the swimmers at the deep end. The instructor walked over to me and without so much as uttering a word, pushed me into the water, where I spent the next four hours dodging a pole each time I swam to the side and grabbed the ledge in an attempt to rest. Because I was black, I wasn't supposed to be a good swimmer and didn't have enough sense to go along with the instructor's expectations.

Another fun day for me occurred when we went for hand to hand combat instructions. During the first week at boot camp, in a question and answer period, I made the mistake of letting it be known that I had studied karate during my former life as a civilian and was pretty good at it. My drill instructors confirmed how good I was by taking me into the hallway one evening and making me give them a demonstration. I remember them smiling at each other and one remarked, "Hand to hand combat class should be fun."

I forgot about his remark until the day came for hand to hand combat training. We were seated in a semicircle in front of the training mats. After a preliminary lecture and the presentation of a few basic principles by the three instructors present, the head instructor called for a "volunteer". No one budged. SSgt. Sargen walked to where I sat and gave me a nudge. I took the hint, stood up and stepped onto the mat. SSgt. Jarrell called to the head self-defense instructor, who told one of his assistants to carry on and headed to where he stood. I took a quick look at our other DIs, standing off to the side. They were smirking to the point of almost giggling.

The assistant self-defense instructor started the lesson by giving a short lecture on how important it was to learn how to disarm someone with your bare hands. With the aid of another instructor, he slowly demonstrated the correct procedure for disarming someone with a knife. After they went through the technique twice, one of the instructors stepped back. The other one launched at me with a fake knife in his hand.

The object of his surprise attack was to see if I had been paying attention to the lesson just given. I quickly stepped to the side, grabbed his wrist and in a sweeping motion, flipped

30

him onto the mat, locking his arm in a position that would have allowed me to break it with a minimum of effort.

Well, you can imagine the surprised look on his face. It was obvious to him and the other instructors that my defense against his attack was a lot more deadly than the technique that had just been demonstrated. I turned to my drill instructors. All four were rolling with laughter. The instructor, who had just been embarrassed, was back on his feet, his face red as a beet. It was the first time in boot camp I can remember the whole platoon laughing and the DIs not cutting it short.

The only ones who weren't laughing were the head self-defense instructor and the assistant I had just thrown. Even the third instructor was working hard at containing his obvious desire to join in the laughter.

By the end of the eighth week of boot camp, we had come a long way. We learned to march as a team. God only knows how many miles we ran and marched. We learned how to use our rifles, our bayonets, how to fight with pugil sticks, and we could pitch a tent with the greatest of ease. When we took our physical readiness test, we were all quite surprised to see how conditioned we had become. The many hours of physical training had paid off.

A few days later, eight long, hard weeks of work and training came to an end. A goal that had at times seemed so unattainable had finally been achieved. It was graduation day. I stood at attention during Final Review, and I thought back over the hardships and trials we all had overcome. I retraced the past eight weeks of intensive training, and felt proud. I had just completed eight weeks of the hardest physical training of my life. I didn't just complete boot camp; I finished at the top of my platoon, and was promoted to Private First Class. I had arrived at Parris Island a lowly civilian and was leaving a UNITED STATES MARINE.

CHAPTER FOUR

The hardest part of Marine Corps training was having to go so long without leave; eight weeks without a break. The day after graduation from Boot Camp, our platoon was, for the most part, broken up. Each of us, now full-fledged Marines, were given orders to various Marine Corps training schools.

At least half of us were ordered to undergo infantry training at Camp Lejune in North Carolina. We had been classified as 0311's or Grunts, the pride of the Marine Corps. Grunt, another strange nick name, stood for infantryman or rifleman. What it actually meant was that we would soon be getting our asses shot at in the jungles of Vietnam. Training to become a combat infantryman meant another eight weeks of training.

From day one of our arrival at Camp Lejune, a lot of energy was pumped into convincing us that it was an honor to have been chosen to become grunts. We were reminded that it was the function of the rest of the Marine Corps to provide us with all the support we needed to do our job.

The schedule and intensity of training at Camp Lejune was almost as rigid and strenuous as that at Parris Island. The biggest difference was that we were treated with some dignity because we were now Marines. We had several weekends off and were allowed to visit the Post Exchange. We could also move freely around the area immediately surrounding our barracks in what little spare time we had. All in all, it wasn't that bad.

Staff Sergeant Jones who was in charge of our platoon was an okay guy, with a strange sense of humor. He was extremely perceptive and could tell when things were exceptionally rough for us. It was at those times he always managed to tell a story, or pull off some stunt that would ease the pressure and make us smile for a while. He had been to Vietnam twice. He took his job of guiding us through infantry training, as a serious mission. The one thing he kept emphasizing was that if we were to survive in Vietnam, we had to develop a sense of humor and hold onto it.

At the time, few of us could figure out why he stressed that so much. Once I arrived in Vietnam a few months later, I found out why it was important. To this day, I thank SSgt. Jones for making his point so forcefully.

The bulk of our training at Camp Lejune dealt with preparing us for actual combat. We learned how to handle such necessary items of warfare as the hand grenade. It was on the grenade range we learned that those soldiers on the silver screen were full of shit when they stuck the safety pin of a hand grenade between their teeth, yanked it out, then tossed the grenade with pinpoint accuracy at the enemy. We learned that because of a Marine in our regiment, who must have watched one too many John Wayne movies.

Though we were given careful instructions on the proper way to pull the safety pin of a hand grenade, this Marine decided to do it his own way. When it was his turn to throw a grenade, before the instructor could stop him, he placed the

34

safety pin between his teeth and began to yank away. He was successful in removing the pin from the handle. However, the ensuing pain from a cracked tooth caused him to drop the live grenade into the pits as he grabbed his mouth and screamed in pain. The only thing that saved him was the instructor's lightning reflex.

With almost blinding speed, the instructor reached for the grenade and sounded the alarm, warning everyone there was a live one in the pits. He immediately tossed the grenade out of the pit and dropped to the ground, pulling the fool who dropped the grenade down with him. After the grenade exploded, it took at least three other instructors to pull the sergeant off John Wayne, Jr. The instructor was screaming and punching him silly.

"Eighteen months in Vietnam, not a scratch, and some asshole like you tries to blow me away."

I'll bet you that "John Wayne Jr.," a newly acquired nickname, which stuck with him for the remainder of infantry training, never watched another John Wayne movie as long as he lived.

Another fun-filled day at infantry training school was our experience with the gas chamber. We spent several hours learning all about chemical warfare and the proper use of a gas mask. After the lecture, we were each issued a mask, marched out of the classroom and herded into a large, empty windowless building. It didn't take much brains to guess what was about to happen.

It soon became clear that most of my fellow trainees either were asleep in class a few minutes earlier, or were too slow to anticipate what was next. Once the last trainee entered the building, the instructor who had led us in quickly darted back

35

out the door, and slammed it behind him. No sooner than he had done this, than I heard what sounded like shutters sliding in place outside the building's exits. In anticipation of what was to come, several of us quickly placed our hands on our gas masks and waited. Sure enough, a few seconds later, a burst of gas shot into the room. I took in a deep breath, held it, removed my mask from my web belt and placed it over my head. Next, I adjusted the straps, blew out my breath to clear the mask and began to breathe in. It was a relief to find that my mask worked so well. Through the cloud of gas I could see some of my fellow trainees who had blown it. They were gagging and coughing all over the place. The guy next to me was really freaking out. I was trying to help him get his mask on when I heard the shutters being rolled up.

A few moments later, a door at the far end of the building swung open. The panic-stricken trainees were setting new world track and field records. They dashed for the exit, hurdling over others who were on their knees coughing and regurgitating. Those who successfully made it through the exercise slowly strolled out of the building. Outside, some were busy wiping their mouths from throwing up while others still gagged and coughed. The instructors were laughing almost uncontrollably. A few hospital corpsmen moved among us to make sure everyone was okay. The suffering was assured they would be all right in a few minutes.

Afterward, we got the standard lecture on how a good seventy percent of us would now be dead if it had been an actual gas attack. I remarked to a few of my fellow Marines within earshot that this was the sixties and if it were a real attack, we would probably all be dead from the gas that would have been used on us. I had serious doubts that the masks we had been issued would have done much good against the deadly chemicals available in this day and age. They nodded their heads in agreement and laughed. The instructor continued to stress how the gas mask could one day save our lives in combat. I just figured that old traditions died hard in the Marine Corps. I also doubted that if gas was ever used against us in Vietnam that it would be as mild as tear gas.

Several days of our training was devoted to learning how to survive off the land. We learned how to tell a poisonous snake from a nonpoisonous one; a process that usually called for you to get close enough to kiss the snake in question to spot the identifying signs. I had never run up on a snake growing up in Harlem. In fact, the only reptiles I had ever seen were behind glass cages at the Bronx Zoo. Snakes didn't phase me one way or the other. I was really surprised that, as a black man, I was supposed to be afraid of them. Now that may sound like a strange statement to make, but it turned out to be true of at least eighty percent of the black trainees present that day. The instructors knew it, too. They took great delight in throwing a couple of snakes at several black trainees who jumped back as far and as fast as their legs would carry them.

The second day of survival training proved to be just as amusing. Right after breakfast, each of us was given the cutest, little rabbit you ever wanted to see. We were told to hold onto our new pets. A few hours later, seventy-five of us were seated in bleachers, listening to a lecture on how the rabbit could be our best friend in the wilderness. We listened intently while petting them. The stroking stopped abruptly when the instructor blurted out, "The rabbit serves many useful purposes. One of which is, it's a great source of food."

Without saying another word, the instructor grabbed the rabbit he was stroking by its feet and gave it a sharp karate chop to the back of the neck. The squirming animal went limp, and blood began dripping from its mouth. Before you knew it, there were at least sixty-five rabbits scurrying for freedom. Most of us released the rabbits we had been holding, as though programmed to do so.

Once things got somewhat back to normal, the instructor hung the rabbit from a string tied to a pole and proceeded to show us how to skin and clean it for eating. Many of the trainees gagged and frowned. Here we were big bad Marines, shuddering at the sight of a rabbit being skinned. One instructor, with a somewhat warped sense of humor, thought that it was fun to throw the rabbit guts into the bleachers. You should have seen how quick our reflexes had become from all our training. Skillfully, we weaved and bobbed to avoid being hit by the various parts of the rabbit's insides. Shortly afterward, we were each given another live rabbit, which we had to kill and skin. It wasn't that difficult to do, since we hadn't petted and befriended the second batch.

It was during infantry training that I came to understand why the number of civilians accidentally shot by U.S. servicemen in Vietnam was so high. We had to go through a course similar to the ones shown on television police serials. It consisted of a series of targets, which sporadically popped up while we slowly moved along a trail. The targets were of silhouettes of a variety of people. Some were of women, children and unarmed civilian men. Others were of armed women and men. When a silhouette popped up we had a second to identify it as friend or foe. If we thought it was a foe, we were to shoot it. I thought of all the stories about American troops shooting civilians in Vietnam. Here we were shooting countless, friendly silhouettes in training, and weren't faced with a life or death situation. It was easy to understand how you could accidentally kill an innocent civilian in war. Later, I would learn that it was especially easy to make such a mistake when the enemy didn't parade around in uniforms, which clearly identified them.

The main object of infantry training school was to teach you how to become an efficient and thorough killing machine. We were drilled and re-drilled in all sorts of combat skills. Although we were constantly reminded that we would soon be at it for real, I doubt that most of us gave it much thought then. Rarely did the subject of Vietnam come up in conversations during our free time. Rumors had begun to circulate that newly elected President Nixon would soon start bringing the troops home from the war. Except for a few gung-ho sickies, we all hoped it was true, and that we would not have to go off to war. Still, we took our training seriously.

Since Camp Lejuene is the Marine Corps' main stateside base, we would often see and meet Marines who had been to Vietnam. Several were still recovering from wounds received during their tour. "Tour in Vietnam." Isn't that a pleasant way to describe getting your ass shot at and rocketed for thirteen months. With few exceptions, most of the Vietnam veterans I met while in training didn't have any desire to return. They were just glad to have made it back home in one piece.

A few days before our training was over, the day that we had waited for was finally at hand. Our orders had arrived. We gathered around SSgt. Jones, who had so dutifully guided us through our training. Slowly, he read our orders. The atmosphere was equivalent to what you would expect at a lottery drawing with a twenty million dollar payoff. SSgt. Jones read off the first group of names and orders. They were to report back to Camp Lejuene after leave and join the Sixth Marines, who were scheduled to leave for the Mediterranean in two months.

The rest of us began to feel somewhat relieved. A Mediterranean cruise was choice duty. One of the trainees, whose name had just been read, was heard saying, "God bless Nixon," as he jumped for joy and quickly ran outside. The rest of us waited, hoping to be assigned anywhere but Vietnam. Our momentary relief ceased after SSgt. Jones read off the next twenty-five names, which included mine, and said the following, "Your orders read: ground forces, the Pacific." In plain English that meant Vietnam. A hushed silence descended on us. We looked at each other, then back at SSgt. Jones, hoping this was just another display of his sense of humor. It wasn't.

We didn't wait around to hear anyone else's orders. We left the room and milled around outside the barracks. Reality had finally caught up with us. Soon, all the training we had undergone the past four months would be tested. For the past few years, I'd seen the casualty figures headlined daily across the newspapers. "176 U.S. servicemen and 700 Viet Cong killed this week," was only one of the many headlines. I had seen the war almost nightly on the television screen. The networks seemed to delight in showing gruesome footage of men maimed in battle and shots of suffering civilians crying for their dead and injured family members and friends. Soon, it would no longer be just be a vision coming through the picture tube. It would be my reality, my nightmare.

I imagined that most of us were thinking similar thoughts at the moment. It was clear that some of us would return physically untouched by the war; some would come back injured and crippled. Others would be missing one or more limbs. A few would return in that feared green plastic bag inside a flag-draped, cold, silver metal box with our dog tags locked tightly between our teeth. From what I had seen and heard from the combat veterans I met over the past few weeks, I knew one thing for sure. All who returned alive would carry the mental scars of the war with us for a long time, if not the rest of our lives.

Training was over a few days later. Slightly more than sixteen weeks after I left New York a lowly civilian, I was transformed into a United Stated Marine Corps Rifleman; a highly skilled killer. My upcoming tour in Vietnam would provide me with the opportunity to test my newly acquired skills. At least that was what I was led to believe. I would soon find out that survival in Vietnam depended a good deal more on luck than the training I had just completed.

Saying goodbye to guys I had become so close to was difficult. Those of us who lived near each other exchanged addresses and made plans to catch up with one another while on leave. Those of us with the same orders just said, "I'll see you in a month in California."

California was the last stop before you embarked on your tour in Vietnam. That last day at Camp Lejuene was the last time I would ever see most of my fellow trainees. In fact, during my remaining fifteen months on active duty, I only saw about a dozen of them again. While on leave, I only contacted one person, a guy from Newark, New Jersey, with whom I had become fairly close friends during the last few weeks of training. We hung out a couple of times at the beginning of our leave. A few months later, in Vietnam, I learned he was killed in action. To this day, whenever I think of him, I hurt all over again. He was a swell person.

Several hours after I bid my comrades farewell, I was seated aboard a Greyhound bus headed home. I spent most of the trip to New York thinking about my past and planning every minute of my leave. If this was to be the last time, I ever saw home, I would enjoy every second of it. I decided I wouldn't think about Vietnam again until I was there. Besides, I had received the best training possible. I decided to take a nap.

Sleep always seemed to speed up a long trip. I made myself comfortable and again began to wonder what had been cut from my training in boot camp.

CHAPTER FIVE

arrived at Camp Pendleton in early May. It was my first trip to California, and I was glad to find it would be at least ten days before I left for Vietnam. The Marine Corps was pretty decent in the way it treated those of us who were headed for the ground forces in the Pacific. We were assigned to light duty and had plenty of free time.

I managed to see a lot of California while awaiting my final orders. However, although I didn't drink, one thing about my stay in California annoyed me. I was born and raised in New York and able to drink liquor legally since the age of eighteen, if I wanted to indulge. I was old enough to be sent overseas to a foreign land to fight a war "to help stop the spread of Communism," and maybe get killed in the process, yet I wasn't old enough to legally have a drink in California.

While there, I witnessed several fights sparked by the drinking laws. Imagine how returning veterans reacted after surviving the horrors of war when they went into a club or bar and were told they were too young to drink.

One particular incident still stands out clearly in my mind. One evening, I was walking past a popular bar in San Diego, when suddenly a body came flying through the tavern's front window. A few seconds later, a Marine in uniform came rushing out the door and began beating on the bartender who had just been hurled through the window. He was beating on the helpless man as though he had suddenly gone mad. He probably had.

Several other Marines followed him out of the tavern and wrestled him away from his victim before he could inflict more suffering. I couldn't help but notice that the Marine, who had been pounding on the helpless bartender, had one arm in a cast, several bandages on his face and a chest full of decorations. His friends quickly whisked him into a car parked nearby and sped off.

A few minutes later, both the local and military police arrived and I listened as the injured bartender explained to the officers what had just happened. It seemed that when the Marine asked for a drink, the bartender asked him for his identification card. Upon examining it, he informed the Marine that in California you had to be twenty-one to drink alcohol. According to the bartender, the Marine then began shouting something about Vietnam and a few choice obscenities, then before he knew it, the Marine reached across the bar and yanked him over it. Before he could utter a word or defend himself, the Marine hurled him through the window. At that point in his story, I simply shook my head and continued on my way.

Although I didn't drink then, I felt that before I returned from Vietnam, I probably would. I also realized that I would also be too young to legally drink in a lot of states when I returned the following year. Physically, I would be twenty years old, but I knew that mentally and emotionally I would be much older. I imagined I too would be outraged, if I were refused a drink upon my return to the states.

The ten days I spent in California passed quickly. I spent the entire day before I was scheduled to ship out for Vietnam in solitude on the beach, watching the gentle, rolling waves of the Pacific Ocean break against the shore. "Shipping out" was just another one of those cute Marine Corps terms that floated around. Actually, I would be flying out on a United Airlines jet. I smiled at that thought as I sat listening to the sound of the surf. I would arrive in Vietnam aboard an ordinary commercial aircraft, as though I were going on a vacation or something.

In boot camp and infantry training school, we had been sheltered from most of the news about the war and the increasing demonstrations against our involvement in Vietnam. While on leave, I spent a lot of time catching up on the developments about the war both in Vietnam and on the home front. I read about the Tet Offensive, and for the first time, wondered what the war was all about. After reading about Tet, several questions came to mind. How could the enemy move so much equipment and so many men undetected? Who were we really fighting?

It was apparent there was a lot more happening over there than we were being told. I began to think that maybe there was something to what McGovern and a few other elected officials had been saying, "We had no business in Vietnam. We couldn't win, and we needed to get out immediately."

Perhaps my former classmates, some of whom went to great lengths to try to convince me that I should desert and flee to Canada while I was still on leave, had a good idea. But, desertion was never really a consideration. I came this far, and for me, there was no turning back. Anyway, my brother had served a tour and a half in Vietnam, and I never heard him complain about having been there. Besides, a good friend of mine whom I admired very much was now over there. He objected to killing, but had a strong sense of duty. Instead of protesting being drafted, he opted to become a medic. I had just mailed a letter to him that morning. We planned to catch up with each other once I arrived in country. "In country" was another way of saying in Vietnam.

I sat in the sand, lost in my thoughts for several hours. By the end of the day, I had decided that it was a little too late for me to begin questioning whether I thought the war was right or wrong. For the next thirteen months, I would push that question out of my mind. I would concentrate on two things once I arrived in Vietnam; surviving and getting home in one piece would be my main objectives.

I remained on the beach until a few minutes past sunset. There was something magical about the sunset that evening. I found it comforting. I walked away from the beach promising myself I would come back to that very spot and watch the sunset again, the first opportunity I had after I returned to the states.

After returning to Camp Pendleton, the first thing I did was telephone home. I was beginning to get nervous. I needed to hear a few familiar voices. After I spoke with several family members, I called my girlfriend. It's amazing how a friendly voice can soothe one's nerves. I listened to her tell me how much she loved me and couldn't wait until I returned to her. It felt good to hear that, but I knew although she meant it at that moment, it wouldn't be the case in a few months. I had already convinced myself that I would receive that dreaded "Dear John" letter. I had heard numerous stories of how men went out and committed suicide after receiving one. Barbara

46

and I had been going together for just over two years. She was my first girlfriend, and I was her first boyfriend. I cared for her dearly and knew I meant a great deal to her. We had experienced a lot together.

Still, I felt a need to protect myself, so I convinced myself that the relationship didn't mean that much to me. I wasn't going to allow myself to be hurt when I received my Dear John letter. To this day, I thank her for not sending one. Instead, she just stopped writing halfway through my tour in Vietnam. After I hung up, I thought of the good times that she and I had shared, then decided to put her out of my mind. I don't need distractions, I thought on my way to the barracks. When I reached the barracks, I finished packing my gear, took a shower, climbed into my bunk and went to sleep. Reveille was at six a.m.

It was ten in the morning when I climbed off the bus at the airport. The last few hours had passed quickly. I hoped the next thirteen months would pass as rapidly. A few minutes later, I was boarding the jet that would carry me on the first part of my flight to Vietnam. The plane would stop in Hawaii, where we would be issued combat fatigues. Shortly thereafter, I would board another chartered commercial aircraft for the remainder of the flight to Vietnam. I paused momentarily before entering the aircraft, turned, and looked around. For a brief moment, I wondered if I would ever see California again. I quickly put that thought out of my mind and mumbled aloud, "You'll be okay. You'll be back before you know it." With that thought fresh in mind, I entered the plane. A stewardess greeted me and told me I was free to take any empty seat.

There was something strange about boarding a commercial aircraft when you knew that you were on your way to fight a war. I looked around for a familiar face. I spotted one Marine with whom I had gone to infantry school. He appeared as glad to see me, as I was, he. Still, it struck me somewhat strange that there was only one person aboard the plane I had trained with. I took the seat next to him and we struck up a conversation.

Not long after I boarded, the aircraft taxied down the runway for takeoff. A few minutes later, we were airborne. There was complete silence aboard the jet as it headed west. The silence remained until the California coast disappeared.

It was weird how, once the coastline seemed to disappear, so did the tension aboard the aircraft. I remember vividly how the atmosphere aboard the plane seemed to go from gloomy to almost festive. There were a few Vietnam veterans aboard and they delighted in telling war stories in an attempt to frighten those of us whom would be arriving in country for the first time.

From what I managed to pick up from the various conversations, Vietnam seemed like a strange kind of place. Stranger than I had imagined it to be. I found it particularly bizarre when I overheard two corporals, sitting directly in front of me, talking about how they couldn't wait to get back to Da Nang. Later, during the flight, I found out they were MPs and had been stationed in Da Nang during their first tour. They already knew they were being reassigned there. At the time, I couldn't figure out what they seemed so delighted about. Once I had the opportunity to go on leave a few months later I found out what a wild and fascinating place

Da Nang was. Listening to them, I couldn't help but hope that I would also be assigned there.

It was early afternoon when we landed in Hawaii. I was disappointed when I found out I wouldn't be there long. I left the plane and boarded a waiting bus for the Marine Corps base, where I was issued my combat fatigues and other basic equipment. Those of us scheduled to continue our journey that evening were restricted to the base. For lack of anything else to do, I spent the next several hours roaming aimlessly around the base.

Less than eight hours after my arrival in Hawaii, I was seated aboard a World Airways jet for the final leg of the trip. It was late evening, and the sun was just starting to disappear as the plane took off. The horizon was a mixture of yellow and deep orange, as the sun slowly blended into the ocean in the distance. Our flight was scheduled to touch down in Vietnam sometime in the early a.m. Before boarding the plane, I had found out that we would land in Da Nang. Maybe I would still get lucky and be assigned there. It was a choice duty station, judging by all the stories I had heard over the past few days. Returning veterans readily compared it to New York. Everyone had such a wild impression of what life in New York was like.

I sat wondering what was in store for me in a few hours when the Marine next to me interrupted my thoughts.

"Have you taken a good look at the stewardesses? They all look like combat veterans." He frowned and shook his head.

"I wouldn't go so far as to say they look like combat vets, but they sure don't look like what you would expect your average stewardess to look like," was my reply.

49

"Tell me about it. The least they could have done was to send us off with a few really fine babes." I didn't respond to his last remarks aloud. Instead, I thought to myself. Here this dude is on his way to fight a war and all he's concerned with is how the stewardesses look.

After my brief conversation, I studied several attendants for a long time. Suddenly, I began to realize that if you looked past what you could see at a glance, you would notice something different about them. They were every bit as pretty as one would expect, made up, or otherwise. What was different about them was the look on their faces. Although they tried to smile and seem pleasant, I sensed it was difficult for them.

After we were airborne a few hours and most of the Marines aboard had fallen asleep, I climbed out of my seat, walked to the front of the cabin and approached two of the stewardesses, standing in the galley, chatting with each other. "Excuse me?"

"Yes?" replied one.

"Could I talk with you a few minutes?"

"Sure," she responded. The other nodded her head in agreement.

"Have you flown this route for very long?"

"I've been on this run for around four months now." "This is my fifth trip into Da Nang," answered the other. We continued our conversation, exchanging bits of personal information. After a few minutes of friendly chatting, I asked a pointed question. "Is it difficult for you to make this run, knowing that many the guys aboard each trip won't be returning home?"

50

"Why do you ask that?"

"Because I couldn't help but notice that neither of you were really smiling. I could tell you were forcing a grin when you welcomed us on the plane."

"You don't think about things like that. If you did, you wouldn't be able to do your job."

The second stewardess chimed in. "The flights over aren't so bad. It's the return runs that break your heart. Most of these guys aboard now are full of life. It's like they don't have a care in the world. The guys we pick up for the return flight home have a different look. Although most of them are happy to go home, there is a look of sadness etched on many of their faces, like a part of their life had been stripped away. It's so hard to keep from crying when they board the plane. I think, because of that, this is going to be my last run on this route."

"Mine too," replied the other stewardess.

We continued to talk for a while before I returned to my seat. A few minutes later, one of them came over and asked if I would like them to write. She informed me that they never exchanged addresses with any of the guys aboard their flights before because they felt it best not to know if they made it through the war okay or not. "My friend and I think you're special. It would be nice if the three of us got together when you return," she added. Both stewardesses were based in Los Angeles and promised me a party to celebrate my return. I thought that was a great idea, so we exchanged addresses.

After she left, I neatly folded the piece of paper with their addresses on it, removed my wallet from my pocket and tucked it securely inside. Returning my wallet to my pocket,

I smiled and looked around the plane. Most of my fellow passengers were in a deep state of sleep. A couple were writing letters, while a few stared out the windows at the blackened night. My anxiety level was much too high for me to fall asleep, so I reached into my handbag and pulled out a copy of The Adventures of Huckleberry Finn. It was my favorite book.

When I finished reading about Huck's adventures once again, I closed the book, got up, and approached one of the stewardesses who had befriended me. "I want you to hold this for me, until I get back," I said, as I handed her the book.

"Why?" she asked.

"Because I heard it rains a lot over there and I don't want it to get wet," I replied. We shared a light laugh. She took the book, leaned over and gave me a gentle kiss on my check. I returned to my seat, still smiling. I made myself comfortable. In a few hours, my time in hell would begin.

CHAPTER SIX

We'll be landing at Da Nang airport in a few minutes. At this time, the Captain has asked that you extinguish all smoking materials, return your seats to the upright position and make sure your seat belts are fastened."

The stewardess' voice over the intercom woke me up from a deep sleep. I wiped the sleep from the corner of my eyes with one hand and with the other, pushed the button returning my seat to the upright position. I pressed my face against the small window and could not believe what I saw. Below was the most beautiful landscape I had ever seen.

The lush green vegetation and deep blue rivers seemed unreal. It looked like a picture painted by one of the great masters. From the air, you couldn't see the hundreds of bomb craters that became evident once you went on your first patrol.

Vietnam from the air made it difficult to imagine that death was everywhere on the ground below. It was easy to forget that the deep green jungles, which looked so inviting from high above, were the same places where so many had died. The same jungle where, maybe, you would "buy it." Another cute expression.

"To "buy it" meant to be killed in combat.

Fifteen minutes after the stewardess made her final announcement we were on the ground and departing the aircraft. I stopped at the exit long enough to say goodbye to the stewardesses and told them to start planning my party immediately after they got back. They smiled, then hugged me simultaneously. One gave me her scarf for good luck. The other unhooked a medallion she was wearing and handed it to me. She held tightly onto my hand for a brief moment before she bent over and kissed me.

"I'll see you at the party."

"You sure will," I replied.

I smiled, winked at the two of them and departed the plane.

Once on the ground, a Marine greeted me and told me to report to a large hanger marked number twelve just outside the airport gates. I lifted my seabag, threw it onto my shoulder, picked up my handbag and headed for the hanger. I glanced back at the plane. The two stewardesses stood in the exit, waving goodbye to everyone. They looked in my direction, saw me, raised their thumbs and gave me the A-okay signal. I nodded my head in acknowledgement, turned and headed across the airfield to the airport exit.

Before I walked through the gates, I paused and looked around. It was weird. Da Nang airport reminded me of La Guardia Airport back in New York. There were several commercial passenger planes parked around the field. Several large cargo planes, both military and commercial, were also parked outside hangers. Behind the main field were dozens of F-4 jet fighters and an assortment of helicopters. It was only seven a.m., and already the sun was beating down unmercifully. It wasn't what I expected. Except for the faint sounds of a few explosions in the distance, it was quiet and somewhat peaceful.

It took me a couple of minutes to reach hanger twelve. Once inside, I dropped my seabag and walked to a desk where a sergeant was seated. Without looking up, he stuck out his hand and asked for my orders. I handed them to him and surveyed the area. The hanger was bursting with activity. Dozens of identical desks were lined up and, in front of each, a Marine stood awaiting his assignment. The sergeant's voice startled me. "Hey Calvin, they sent us a bunch of babies this trip," he shouted to another sergeant seated behind the desk to his right. He looked up at me and I looked down at him. "How old are you son?"

"Nineteen," I replied in a deep voice.

"Get the hell out of here! You can tell me the truth, sonny."

You lied about your age to get in the Marines, didn't you?" "No sergeant. I'm nineteen," I responded firmly.

"Get the hell out of here!" he repeated.

He shook his head, picked up a rubber stamp, and stamped my orders. He then shouted to a Lance Corporal standing off to the side of the row of desks.

"Show baby face here where he can draw his gear and where to find the truck leaving for One-Nine."

The Lance Corporal motioned for me to follow him. I picked up my belongings and ran to catch up. When I did, he looked at me, shook his head and mumbled something.

"Excuse me. Did you say something to me?" "Walking Dead," was his answer.

"Walking Dead?" I asked again with a keen interest.

55

"First Battalion-Ninth Marines, the Walking Dead," was all he said. By now my curiosity was really aroused. I continued to question him.

"Exactly what does that mean?"

"It means you've just been fucked." Friendly guy, I thought.

We stopped in front of a large counter. Behind it, there were racks and racks filled with all sorts of weapons.

"What have we here?" asked the smiling sergeant on the other side of the counter.

"0311," replied my escort.

He then snatched the folder containing my orders from me, tore off a copy, handed it to the supply sergeant and thrust the folder back at me.

"After you draw your weapon, you'll see a bunch of trucks outside to your left. Find the one marked One-Nine and report to the driver," my escort instructed me.

"Thanks," I replied.

"Don't mention it. It's been my pleasure." He snickered again, and walked away.

I turned to the sergeant behind the counter. He reached over the counter, and handed me a rifle and a receipt to fill out. I stood there in total bewilderment, staring at the rifle. I recognized it from a few pictures I had seen back in the states. It was an M-16. The puzzled look on my face must have been real obvious because before I could say a word, the sergeant spoke.

"It's an M-16."

"But I trained with an M-14," I replied, baffled. "I've never fired an M-16 before."

"Don't worry about it. Where you're headed you'll get plenty of on the job training."

"Where's One-Nine located?"

"About as far north as you can go without accidentally stumbling into Uncle Ho's living room."

"What does that mean?" I asked respectfully.

"It means you are about to find yourself in the thick of this shit. One-Nine is in Quang Tri Province. Vandergrift Combat base. In the Ashau Valley to be exact."

Since I wasn't familiar with the Vietnam geography, his answer was Greek to me, so I continued to question him.

"What does all that really mean?"

"What it really means, is that you've had the misfortune of being assigned to one of the toughest outfits in the Corps.

One-Nine has had its share of fighting. They are nicknamed the Walking Dead because we play a little psychological game with the enemy. As quickly as they do a job on One-Nine, we replace the dead and wounded and send One-Nine right back out. It confuses the hell out of them. They think they are seeing ghosts. A few times, the North Vietnamese have damn near wiped out One-Nine. But, quicker than they can say "Hanoi," we replace each dead and wounded man with a nice fresh Marine... just like you. When Charlie looks around, One-Nine is hot on his ass again."

At that point, I didn't know if he was kidding in an attempt to scare me a little more than I already was, or if he was serious. Without asking any more questions, I gathered up the ammunition magazines along with the ammo he had placed on the counter, shoved them into my pockets and grabbed my unfamiliar rifle by it's strange looking, built-on handle.

Next, I picked up my personal belongings and headed for the truck, which was to take me to join the ranks of the Walking Dead. I strolled toward the hangar exit somewhat freaked out by the fact the Marine Corps had switched from the M-14 rifle to the M-16 in the middle of the war.

Someone had to know months ago that they were going to make the switch. They could have trained us with the M-16. Those thoughts disturbed me. I noticed immediately that the M-16 was much lighter than the M-14. That was a definite plus.

Once outside, I had no trouble finding the truck that would take me to my unit. There was a large, red sign strapped to the front of the truck. In the center was a drawing, in white, of a skull with a set of crossed bones just below it. To the left of the skull was a large number one, a slash mark and the number nine. To the right of the skull were the words "Walking Dead." Later I learned that the sign was a blow-up of One-Nine's unofficial insignia. Its official insignia was a design resembling a badge, with a large number nine in the middle. Through the center of the number there was a lightning bolt. Below the badge was a scroll with the words One-Nine written across it. I approached a corporal standing next to the driver's side of the truck.

"Are you the driver?" "Sure am."

"I was instructed to report to you. Here are my orders."

"Don't need them. Climb aboard. We're pulling out in a few minutes."

I walked around to the rear of the truck, threw my seabag and handbag in, then climbed inside. The canvas covering was drawn back, permitting an unobstructed view of the surroundings. Four other Marines were already seated in the rear of the truck. We introduced ourselves and chatted while we waited to pull off. It was reassuring to know that I wasn't the only one who was nervous and a bit frightened. If all that crap about One-Nine we had heard since being assigned was just a crock of bullshit meant to scare us newcomers, it had worked. Within five minutes of my climbing aboard the truck, seven other newly arrived Marines had joined us. The driver stepped to the rear, and read our names off a sheet of paper. "Yo," we answered one by one. He checked off each of our names, and began issuing instructions.

"We will be heading north to your new home, as part of a convoy. Charlie has been pretty active around here the past few days. The last two convoys out of here were ambushed. Now if you gentlemen will load your magazines, lock and load your weapons, we'll be on our way. Keep alert and let's hope we have a pleasant trip. Enjoy the scenery."

Can you imagine? Here we were a dozen young, untried, nervous, and slightly scared Marines on our way to join the ranks of the infamous Walking Dead, being told that we might wind up in a firefight before we even joined up with our unit. A firefight was just more military jargon. It meant you were being shot at and, if you were lucky, you got to shoot back. I suspect the term originated from firing your weapons while fighting. Naturally, none of us hesitated in pulling out the boxes of ammunition and magazines (ammo clips) we had been issued a few minutes earlier. Quick as a wink, we loaded our magazines and locked and loaded our rifles.

A few minutes later, the truck jerked forward and began to roll. It took up a position near the end of the convoy. To our rear, was a jeep with a fifty-caliber machine gun mounted on top. The convoy slowly headed north, and for the first time, I began to believe I was in the middle of a war.

The ride from Da Nang to Vandergrift Combat Base was slow and uncomfortable. The convoy seemed to be moving at a snail's pace. It rumbled along, surrounded by a huge cloud of red dust rising from the dry road. A mine sweep was leading the column of trucks. The Viet Cong had increased their mining of the roads lately. Every precaution was taken to avoid any more casualties from trucks being blown to bits after rolling over a mine. Each time we passed a village or a hamlet you could feel the tension mount inside our truck. Our only knowledge about the enemy came from the stories we had heard back in the states. We were told they were nowhere but everywhere, all simultaneously. We expected them to pop out of tunnels and from behind the hamlet and village huts any second.

There was sadness etched in the faces of many of the Vietnamese people we passed along the way. The wide-eyed children, who paraded along the road, moved me. The adults seemed to be oblivious to our passing. Why not? Many of them had seen the French, the Japanese, the French again and now the American troops pass down these same roads on previous occasions. I was amazed at how the Vietnamese people moved along the road with the greatest of ease while we were so cautious.

The farther we traveled, the smaller our convoy got. At several points along our route, trucks pulled away and headed in different directions. They were delivering fresh troops and supplies to various combat bases in the area. Several hours after the convoy left Da Nang, we arrived at our destination, Vandergrift Combat Base, south of the Ashau Valley. Everyone seemed relieved that our trip was peaceful and uninterrupted.

Once the truck stopped, the twelve of us climbed out. It was a depressing place. There were large tents and makeshift barracks scattered everywhere. Between the tents and buildings, there were dozens of trenches surrounded by sandbags. Everything seemed to be covered with a distinctive layer of red dirt. I stood shaking my head in disbelief at what was to be my home. A corporal emerged from a tent a few yards away from where we stood, and casually strolled over to us. "Welcome to your home away from home. Your Hilton in the jungle. If you gentlemen will follow me, I'll help you get squared away." He motioned for us to follow.

The camp was bustling with activity. Around eighty yards to our right, several helicopters were taking off and landing. Ambulances rushed to and from the choppers. What appeared to be wounded or dead Marines were carried from the choppers and others, equipped for combat, climbed aboard. Seconds later, the choppers were airborne. Sounds of an intensive battle could be heard echoing throughout the hills and mountains surrounding the base. Silently, we followed the corporal into the large tent, which served as battalion headquarters. We looked at each other. No words were spoken. The message was clear. Soon it would be our turn to board a chopper, to be whisked off and dropped in the middle of the fighting. Once inside the tent, we were greeted by a Gunnery Sergeant.

"Welcome aboard, gentlemen. You have been lucky enough to be assigned to the meanest and the best fighting unit in this whole damn, rotten stinking war. You'll be fighting alongside some of the bravest men it has been my pleasure to serve with. In a few days, I'm sure I'll be able to say the same about you."

We then handed our service records to him, and were each assigned to a company. I was assigned to Bravo Company of the first battalion and told they were in the field and engaged in some heavy fighting.

"You men will follow Corporal Hastings to the supply tent where you'll draw the rest of your gear, then he'll show you to your company area. There is a small firing range out back. Once you've stowed your gear, I suggest you use it to set your sights and familiarize yourself with your weapon. Have a good day, gentlemen."

We turned, accompanied Cpl. Hastings out of the tent and followed him to another large tent just to the left of headquarters. From inside, we could hear a lot of clatter and screaming. Hastings informed us that this tent was the battalion command post and communications center. We stood in front while Corporal Hastings pointed out various areas of the camp. I ignored him. I was much too busy listening to the sounds of war coming over the radios inside the tent. What sounded like small arms fire, along with various shouting voices could be distinctively heard. Some were screams of pain and others were company commanders and platoon leaders calling for support.

"I've got three wounded men here," someone shouted. "What's taking the chopper so long? I want my wounded out of here!"

Simultaneously over another radio I heard other messages. "The first and second platoons have been caught in a crossfire. Can you bail them out?"

"I read you. We can cover their left flank. Have them fall back." Suddenly, there was a loud explosion, a few moments of silence, and then the radio transmission began again.

"Bravo, can you copy? I repeat, can you copy?"

There was no reply. A few moments later, the same voice could be heard.

"HQ, this is Alpha. We've lost radio contact with Bravo. We are under a rocket attack. Can you arrange for air support?"

"One hot meal coming up. Where do you want it served?" came the reply from inside the tent. Someone, whom I guessed to be the platoon leader, radioed in a set of coordinates. Before I could hear anymore, Cpl. Hastings started walking again and instructed us to follow.

Parts of the interchange I had just overheard kept repeating itself in my mind.

"HQ this is Alpha, we have lost radio contact with Bravo."

Bravo, or what was left of them, was the company I had been assigned to. What have I walked into? I thought, as we reached the supply area.

"Here's where you'll draw your supplies. First, I suggest you report to your company area, drop off your gear, then return here and get outfitted."

After addressing us, Cpl. Hastings pointed in the direction of our various companies, then bade us goodbye.

I deliberately took my time getting to Bravo Company's area. The sounds of war continued to echo in the distance. It was a reality now. Was I prepared to fight? Would I perform as was expected of me? Would I be able to take another human life? Those and countless other questions crossed my mind. When I reached my company headquarters, I stepped inside and reported to the Staff Sergeant seated behind a desk. He shook my hand, welcomed me aboard and told me to follow him. Once outside, he showed me to my tent and told me where I could stow my gear.

"After you pick up your supplies, park your cot in any open space, then report back to me. I'll show you around."

At the supply tent, I was issued standard combat gear, including a helmet, flack jacket, jungle boots, several more magazines, mess gear, a backpack, poncho with liner, a fold up canvas cot and an assortment of other items I would need when I went into the bush. The "bush" was the term for going on a mission or patrol.

Two hours later, I was back in my tent. By now, several other Marines were there. They introduced themselves. Some were replacements, like myself, and a couple were recovering from minor wounds. It was early evening, and by now, the day's casualty figures had begun to come in. It was then that I learned that shortly after noon, One-Nine, notably Bravo Company, had run into a large force of North Vietnamese Regulars (NVA), down by an area known as the Rockpile.

Initially, they were caught by surprise, but successfully managed to engage the North Vietnamese soldiers and fight them off. By late afternoon, they were mopping-up and would return to Vandergrift the next morning. Mopping-up was a nice way of saying there was still a little fighting going on. They would be given a few days to rest and regroup before hitting the bush again. Reports indicated that the Walking Dead had inflicted heavy casualties on the enemy. The operation, code named Apache Snow, was turning into a success. I knew that once Bravo Company re-grouped; I would hit the bush with them. Before I could dwell on what battle would be like, one of the combat veterans in the tent walked over to me and spoke. "Don't think about it. You'll be okay. Come on, let's go have a beer."

Without thinking or answering, I got up, grabbed my rifle and started to follow. He saw me tuck my weapon under my arm, stopped and smiled. "You won't need that. We're pretty secure back here."

That's what you say, I thought. I tightened my grip on my rifle and followed him out of the tent.

CHAPTER SEVEN

By mid-afternoon of my second day in country, the entire battalion had returned from the field. I should say, what was left of them. They had sustained heavy casualties near the Rockpile. Yet, Central Command (I Corps) was calling operation Apache Snow a huge success.

From the looks of the battalion, when they returned from the field, it seemed questionable. The battalion had suffered a casualty rate of almost thirty percent, which included those killed and wounded in action. Bravo Company accounted for a disproportionate number of the battalion's casualty figures, over forty percent. More deaths for the networks to report as part of their weekly live coverage of the war.

It was upsetting to watch the battle-scarred, dirt-covered, and obviously exhausted Marines return to the combat base. The pain and suffering that my fellow Marines had endured on the battlefront was clearly visible. I stood near the landing field, watching helicopter after helicopter land, until the last chopper dropped off its human cargo. I tried hard to imagine what they had just undergone. Until I experienced actual combat first- hand, I knew I couldn't begin to fathom what it would be like. I decided to stall returning to my company area for as long as I could.

How would the men of Bravo Company receive me, I wondered. Surely, at this point, I'm an outsider to these men who have just returned from fighting side by side. Several hours later, I mustered up the courage to return to the tent and introduce myself. Much to my relief, surprise and delight, I was greeted warmly. Within hours, I felt like I'd known several of the men of Bravo Company for a long time.

I was assigned to second squad, first platoon. My platoon leader, Second Lieutenant Smith, always made it a point to check in on the morale of his men after they returned from the bush. He also preferred to meet the new men under his command promptly. The first platoon had been hit pretty hard. They had suffered heavy casualties and were reduced to two squads by the time they returned to Vandergrift. Although everyone tried to be optimistic and cheerful, the sadness that resulted at having lost so many comrades was evident.

At first when Lieutenant Smith entered our tent, carrying two cases of beer, I didn't realize he was the platoon leader. After I heard several men address him by his rank, I immediately stood and snapped to attention. A handful of men snickered.

"Around here, we don't stand on formalities," Lieutenant Smith said. He handed the cases of beer to one of the troops, walked to where I stood, alongside several other newly arrived replacements, and formally introduced himself. Everyone was handed a can of beer, and then the Lieutenant addressed us as a group.

"Let us toast our comrades who fought and died gallantly. May they find everlasting peace. May our wounded recover fully and quickly. Those of us who returned safely are thankful for that. I also raise my drink in a welcome aboard salute to the new men of the first platoon."

That was it, a short but meaningful toast. It was his way of letting us know that although new to the platoon, we were a part of it in every sense. He conversed with a few of the veterans in the tent before bidding everyone goodbye and exiting the tent.

I noticed that Lieutenant Smith wasn't wearing any bars or insignia which showed his rank. In fact, neither was anyone else, except us cherries. My curiosity was raised, and I didn't hesitate to ask about it. The reason made good sense as explained to me. In the bush, you didn't exactly want to advertise who you were. Whenever you went into combat, you made sure the insignias showing your rank, were pinned to the underside of your shirt collar. Since most of the fighting was carried on by small units, knowing who was who, wasn't a problem. You got to know everyone in virtually no time at all. I also found out that at Vandergrift, generally, they didn't stand on formality. Saluting officers was done only when members of the divisional command were visiting the camp from I Corps.

Occasionally, a newly arrived second lieutenant would insist that he be saluted. That usually lasted a day or two, before a senior officer informed him of the folly of his ways. The word "Sir" wasn't heard often around Vandergrift, either. The officers and senior non-commissioned officers were usually addressed by their rank. The rest of the Marines were addressed by their last name or various acquired nicknames. In a combat unit, rank didn't automatically carry respect. Respect was something that was earned on the battlefield. When it came to fighting abilities, there was a great deal of mutual respect between the officers, non-commissioned officers and enlisted personnel at Vandergrift.

Most of the Marines, who had just returned from the bush, spent the remainder of the afternoon cleaning themselves, their gear, and writing letters home. By five that evening, the spirit in the tent had been uplifted, partially aided by the consumption of countless beers. It was during the first day with my company when I noticed something strange. It was apparent that in the bush everyone functioned as a cohesive team and fought bravely alongside one another. Yet, back at the base camp, with few exceptions, the black and white Marines didn't mingle with each other. There seemed to be an unwritten rule against interracial socializing.

The Civil Rights and Black Power movements were in full swing back in the states. It was both interesting and frightening to see how those movements spilled over to life in Vietnam. Men, who just a few short hours earlier had fought side by side without hesitating to put their lives on the line for each other, were now sitting in the same tent, just a few feet from each other, not speaking.

That same evening, I learned that the hostility between the black and white Marines was a lot stronger than I had first suspected. It was close to six p.m. when a few of the black Marines decided to play a game of basketball on a makeshift court behind our tent. Several Marines brought their radios with them and, after tuning into the same station, set the radios in different spots around the court. We were having a good time, half-dancing and half-playing ball. The replacements seemed to be breathing fresh life into the combat veterans. For the moment, the war had disappeared. Suddenly, a shot rang out.

It became instantly evident which of us were combat veterans and which were cherry boys. The veterans immediately dove to the ground. The rest of us stood there momentarily, until several vets began shouting at us to hit the dirt. Without further hesitation, we complied.

"I'm hit!" shouted one of the privates who, seconds earlier, seemed not to have a care in the world. I waited, kissing the dirt, expecting to hear the sounds of continued rifle fire followed by a barrage of mortars and rockets. Neither came. The next sound I heard was a voice that sounded like it was coming from behind a tent, twenty or so yards to the right of the basketball court.

"Fucking niggers!"

At that point, several black Marines carefully crawled to where they had left their forty-fives and grabbed them. Fortunately, before they could return fire, we saw several officers running toward the direction from where the round had been fired. Slowly, we stood up. It was then that I learned, what I momentarily thought was a surprise enemy attack was one of many racial incidents that I would witness while in Vietnam.

An investigation into the incident was launched, but as was expected, nothing resulted from it. The entire episode left me and the other replacements badly shaken. The combat vets seemed to take it in stride. Their nonchalant reaction to the whole affair led me to conclude that what had just occurred wasn't an isolated incident. The Marine who had been struck was just winged in the arm. He was fine after receiving minor medical attention from a corpsman.

A while later, we were back in our tent when the company Gunnery Sargent entered and read off the names of those assigned to guard duty. My name was included. I grabbed my rifle, helmet and flack jacket and followed him, along with three of my comrades. Rows and rows of single-apron triple-concertina and double- apron fence wire surrounded the base perimeter. Between the wire, dozens of claymore mines and flares were attached to trip wires. We were positioned several yards behind the last row, and told to keep alert and not worry. If anyone tried to crawl through the wire, they would trip a claymore mine and blow their ass to kingdom come. If they tripped a flare, the perimeter would light up as though it was midday.

I was paired off with a corporal who had been in country close to a year. He was scheduled to rotate back to the states in thirty days; a short-timer; someone with less than ninety days left to serve in Vietnam. We spent the first few hours engaged in a variety of conversations. He did most of the talking and I did most of the listening. I was fascinated by the stories he told of his tour in Vietnam and glad to hear the war wasn't all fighting and no fun. According to Corporal Johnson, he had more fun during the past eleven months than suffering. Suddenly, in the middle of a sentence, I froze. I heard a strange whistle. I tightened my grip on my rifle and glanced over at Corporal Johnson. Much to my surprise he was smiling. My nervousness amused him.

"Relax, Henry. It's Nguyen."

"Who the hell is Nguyen?"

"He's cool. He's a kid from the village who supplies us with our weed."

I sat there in total disbelief, watching the Vietnamese youth skillfully inch his way through the yards and yards of wire. He didn't even come close to tripping a claymore or setting off a flare. When he reached our position, Johnson handed him a wad of money and Nguyen gave him a medium size bag full of pot. After their exchange, Nguyen turned around and wiggled his way safely back through the maze of wire and explosives. It was unbelievable! Up until that point, Johnson had succeeded in convincing me that we were safe on guard duty. Now, I began to have a few serious doubts. If this little kid could so easily make his way through the perimeter safeguards, how safe were we? Johnson rolled a joint and lit it. He offered me a drag. I declined, informing him that I didn't do drugs. He just smiled and said, "You will before you leave this place, brother. You sure enough will, brother."

No sooner had Johnson taken a last deep drag and extinguished the joint, than the night sky lit up without warning. All hell broke loose on the line. Within seconds, gunfire could be heard, and tracer rounds seen coming from several posts around the perimeter. To our left, the guards opened fire with an M-60 machine gun and didn't stop firing until they emptied a full box of ammo.

After a few moments, someone hollered, "Cease fire! Cease fire!"

Several flares were shot up over the area where the first flare had gone off moments earlier. Tens of thousands of candle power lit up the night sky. My mouth dropped open, and I stared in utter amazement. A tiger was crouched below the barbed wire. Without blinking an eyelash, it turned around and made its way back through the wire. Hundreds of rounds had been fired, and the tiger wasn't even scratched. I turned to Cpl. Johnson. The whole incident hadn't even phased him. Either he knew all along there wasn't anything to be concerned about, or he was too stoned to care. A short while later, Johnson lit another joint and we began talking again.

"When I get back to the real world, look out! I'm going to stay fired-up for the first few weeks, and then I'm going to put all this shit behind me. I should be able to get into Penn State in September. I'm going to become a lawyer."

I sat listening to Johnson while I said a silent prayer for him. I prayed that he would get through his last few days okay, and things would work out for him back in the real world. After witnessing the events of a few hours earlier, I understood why everyone called back home the "real world." From what I had seen so far of what service in Vietnam was like, it seemed more like a dream than reality. A nightmare to be exact.

While on guard duty with Johnson, I learned a little about why there was so much hostility between the black and white Marines. Most of the officers and senior staff NCO's were white southerners and there was something about their tone when they spoke to the black troops that was extremely annoying. Johnson said they acted like it hurt them to have to speak to the black Marines.

He went on to tell me how the black Marines were always getting the short end of the stick. In the eleven months he'd been in Vietnam, he'd seen an awful lot of Marines killed and wounded in battle. He had gathered some statistics on the number of black Marines in Vietnam and kept track of the number of blacks in the Corps. He also made it a point to keep track of the number assigned to the Third Marine Division and the number of black Marines killed or wounded in battle. The figures were way out of line with each other.

The percentage of blacks who wound up on the casualty list was at least two and a half times greater than the number of blacks serving in the Corps, and at least four times larger than the number of black males in the general population back home. It seemed to him that most of the blacks who arrived in country were intentionally assigned to outfits in the thick of it.

Johnson informed me that many of the brothers who had MOS's (Military Occupational Specialties) other than 0311 (Rifleman), were assigned to rifle companies. Meanwhile, a lot of whites who were 0311's, were assigned to service companies and headquarters. What made matters worse was that whenever orders for promotions came down, the whites at headquarters saw to it that they and their buddies got them. As far as he and the other black Marines were concerned, they were being shitted on. He let me know that I would see what he was talking about for myself, once I reached the bush.

I sensed his bitterness and resentment. In fact, Johnson was extremely angry and later I would find out that most of the black Marines felt the same way.

"A lot of them redneck platoon leaders delight in sticking us on point or tail-end Charlie. It's bad enough that they fuck with us in the bush. They fuck with us in the rear, also," he said indignantly.

"Are you referring to what happened this afternoon?" I asked.

"That was light shit. You haven't seen a thing yet." "They'll find out who did it."

"You'd better wake up little brother. In the bush, it's a matter of survival. We fight together because we have to. In the rear, you had better watch your ass closely because these redneck motherfuckers think nothing of blowing it away when they think they can get away with it. I know at least three brothers who were wasted by some redneck. They were listed as killed in action. Don't ever go to the showers at night by yourself. A few brothers have been jumped and beat up pretty bad when they were in there alone at night. In the rear, we look out for each other because it's the only way."

Suddenly, Johnson stopped talking and lit up his third joint of the night. In a few minutes, he was in another world.

I sat listening to the sounds of the night, thinking about everything I had seen since yesterday and what Johnson had just told me. What the hell is happening over here? We were supposed to be at war with the Viet Cong and the North Vietnamese, not with each other. Is everything Johnson told me true? The answers to my questions were evident. The incident on the basketball court, earlier in the day, was enough proof for me.

Johnson was out for the count. I spent the rest of the night sitting in the fox hole, wrapped in my poncho liner, thinking and trying to make sense out of everything. I was also trying to stay warm. The weather in Vietnam was just another weird thing about the war. Although it was somewhere around seventy-five to eighty degrees, I was still pretty chilly. It had been close to one hundred and ten degrees earlier that day. The thirty or so degree drop in temperature could be felt.

The sun began to rise somewhere around five-fifty. I welcomed the first signs of the dawning of a new day. We were scheduled to go off guard duty at six a.m. I reached over and nudged Johnson. Startled by my touch, he jumped up, rifle in hand, poised, ready to shoot. It was my turn to smile. "It's okay! It's morning. We'll be relieved in a few minutes," I quickly shouted at him.

"You scared the shit out of me. I'm sorry I crashed on you. Why didn't you wake me when it was my turn to go on watch?" Johnson sat back down, poured some water from his canteen into his hand and splashed it onto his face.

"It was cool. I wasn't tired. I didn't mind." "Thanks. I owe you one."

"Forget it."

Suddenly, I heard someone approaching from the rear. Quickly, I turned around and, just as I had been trained to do, shouted, "Halt, who goes there?" Johnson began to laugh aloud.

"You'll have to excuse him. It's his first night out," he said to two black Marines, who by now were standing in front of the fox hole. Both of them were laughing, looking at me, and shaking their heads.

"Save anything for me?" one of them asked.

"Sure did," Johnson replied. He reached into his bag of pot and grabbed a handful of the grass.

"Got anything to put it in?"

"Sure enough. How's this?"

One of our reliefs pulled out a box of Kool cigarettes, removed the few remaining cigarettes and handed the open box to Johnson who immediately filled it with pot.

"It's pretty wicked. Don't hurt yourself." "Don't worry, I won't. Later!"

"Later!" Johnson replied.

I watched the three of them give each other the black power handshake that was soon to become another point of controversy in this crazy, mixed-up war. When it was my turn to shake hands and say goodbye, I hoped that I would do it right. I lucked out and got it correct, or at least close enough to correct that they didn't laugh at me again. I bent down and picked up my gear, then Johnson and I started back to the company area. Halfway there, he stopped and started laughing again.

"When you shouted halt, who were you expecting to be coming up from behind you? If it was Charlie, you'd have been dead." We continued toward our tent and I had to laugh at myself. Now that I thought about it, it was pretty funny. By the time I had turned around and shouted, "Halt! Who goes there?" The two Marines were less than five feet away. It was evident who they were. They were both black and over six feet tall. There was no mistaking them for Charlie. We recalled the event with the tiger the night before, and by the time we reached our tent, we were rolling in laughter.

We dropped off our gear, then headed for the showers. I stood soaping myself, thinking about how my heart had raced when the flare first went off the night before. I marveled at how funny the whole thing seemed now. I pulled the chain overhead and the water came pouring down on me, rinsing off the soap. As I dried off, I remembered what I had been told by SSgt. Jones. "Keeping a sense of humor was an important part of survival while in Vietnam."

I made a vow right then to hold onto mine.

CHAPTER EIGHT

My first few days at One-Nine had been interesting, to say the least. My sense of humor and quick wit was a definite plus. Most of the veterans in the regiment took an instant liking to me. I could find a bit of humor in many of the things that went on at Vandergrift and was always quick to joke and share my humorous perspective with everyone. A few of the combat veterans teased me the first time they saw me in all my combat gear. I didn't look like what you would expect a Marine to look like. My entire body weight of one hundred and fifty pounds was stretched out over six feet two inches; two thirds of which was legs. My combat fatigues were a lot looser on me than they were designed to fit, and my flack jacket hung on me with room to spare. I was still incapable of growing facial hair and had a baby face. I looked more like a stretched-out kid playing soldier than I did a real United States Marine. But look like it or not, I was a Marine and, in a few hours, I would find out exactly what that meant.

Sunrise was still a good forty-five or so minutes away. I stood near the helicopter landing field, and the anticipation of what was to soon come brought with it a strange feeling. I wasn't scared at that point, but extremely nervous. In less than a half an hour, we would board the choppers and be lifted off to the bush. The entire regiment was about to begin participation in a new operation, code named Cameron Falls. Intelligence had confirmed a reconnaissance report of a large enemy presence south of Vandergrift. According to the report, the enemy was utilizing a nearby mountain for observation of our combat base and for attacks on convoys and troops along Route 9. As part of the operation, Company B (Bravo Company) and Company C (Charlie Company) were given the assignment of engaging and clearing the enemy out of their mountain positions.

At the same time, the remainder of our battalion, along with the second battalion of the Ninth Marines (2/9), would join up with the U.S. Army and soldiers from the Army of the Republic of Viet-Nam (ARVN) in the area of the old Khe Sanh Combat Base. Their mission was to search the area and clear out any enemy they found. Once that was done, they were to continue north and push the enemy back across the DMZ (Demilitarized Zone). This kind of operation was known as "search and clear." A name with a nice sound to it, but extremely misleading.

Although we were supposed to be seeking out the enemy, if they didn't want to be found, they weren't. From what I had been told by the veteran fighters, we would fight if and only when the Viet Cong or the North Vietnamese wanted to fight. If they felt it was to their advantage, then they would engage us in combat. They would strike first and without warning. On the other hand, if at a given time, they didn't feel they had the element of surprise, they would simply remain in their well concealed positions.

Once we eliminated the enemy from their mountain strongholds, Bravo Company was to serve as a blocking force

for the Army and ARVN units driving north. It was made clear to us that we would have to hold our own. We could expect to be in the field for at least four weeks, during which time we also could expect to be engaged in heavy combat.

Our company commander, Captain Jenkins, knew that most of the units in the area would be engaged in various aspects of operation Cameron Falls. Because of the large size of the operation, if we got into a fix, the nearest support would have to come from over 50 kilometers (as the crow flies). What all that meant was that we were on our own, once we were dropped off.

While we waited for the command to board the choppers our company commander briefed us on our mission. Captain Jenkins was the type of commander that everyone respected and praised. As the senior captain, he would be in command of the two companies. He was what was called a mustanger. That meant that he had started his career in the Marine Corps as an enlisted man and wound up as an officer. I was told and would soon see for myself, that he was one of the best field commanders in the division.

After briefing his officers, Captain Jenkins would address the entire company before each mission. His leadership style was somewhat like that of a football coach. He would fill us in on as much of the details of the mission as he could, then give sort of a pep talk. Today was no different. I listened as he spoke.

"Once we reach our destination, we'll set up camp and then we will begin our patrols."

No sooner had the last words rolled off his lips, than the engines of the helicopters began to churn. The time had arrived. As I boarded the chopper that was to carry my squad

80

and me into combat, I took a good look around the field. What I saw could best be described as an awesome display of power.

Our transport choppers were to be escorted by a dozen Huey Gunships. Hueys were highly maneuverable helicopters, which carried a hell of a lot of fire power. There were several M-60 machine guns mounted on each. They were capable of spraying an area the size of a football field with rounds one inch apart in less than sixty seconds. Knowing you had several Hueys as escorts until you reached the ground offered a false sense of security. At least you felt that you would reach your destination in one piece.

Captain Jenkins informed us that once on the ground, we would operate in platoon-sized reactionary forces, which were platoon-sized groups of Marines who were highly maneuverable and armed with enough fire power to allegedly handle any situation that they ran into. To that end, each platoon was equipped with a minimum of one Marine armed with a grenade launcher (M-72), and one M-60 machine gunner.

Along with our standard gear and supplies, each man in the platoon had to carry either a light assault weapon (LAW), extra grenades for the M-72, or extra ammunition for the M-60. A LAW was a war product of the modern age and designed to be a disposable bazooka. The round it fired was capable of penetrating eleven inches of reinforced concrete.

Although the LAW was designed to be disposable, in actuality we could never dispose of the rocket housing. It was housed in a fiberglass casing. When you pushed a button, the case expanded on both ends. Once you fired the rocket, the housing was supposed to be useless and, as such, discarded.

The entire rocket and its housing weighed only a few pounds, giving it a tremendous advantage over its predecessor, the heavy and cumbersome bazooka. The only flaw with it was that it wasn't as disposable as it was designed to be.

The Viet Cong were quite adept at utilizing our junk. The LAW casing was no exception. They wasted no time in finding out how to use the empty M-72 housing as a weapon against us. The empty housing was just long enough to hold six hand grenades and the Viet Cong made booby traps out of them. They would remove the safety pins from six grenades and carefully insert the explosives in the housing. The diameter was just the right size to prevent the handle of the grenade from springing loose, thereby arming it.

Once the grenades were snugly in position, the VC would close the lid on the end of the M-72 housing. Then they would place it in a tree on an angle with a trip wire attached. If someone had the misfortune of setting off the trip wire, it would pull the lid open, and the six grenades would drop from the housing. Once they slid from the housing, the handles would pop away, arming them. Seconds later, six live and deadly grenades would begin exploding, one right after the other.

A grenade had a killing radius of approximately fifteen feet and a wounding radius of approximately twenty-five feet. The damage done by such a simple, yet effective booby trap was devastating. So, we didn't dispose of the housing once we fired the M-72. For our own safety, we had to carry them back to the rear. There was little doubt that we were better equipped than the enemy. That was our edge. Theirs was that we had to fight them on their territory and their terms.

My thoughts of what was to come were interrupted by a sinking feeling in my stomach as the chopper lifted off. I turned to Corporal Johnson, who was seated to my right. He was my squad leader. I looked at him and couldn't help but think, I hope he takes combat a lot more seriously than he takes guard duty.

Actually, I wasn't that concerned about Johnson's leadership skills. After all, he had survived almost a year in Nam and received several decorations for bravery in the process. A few of the other combat vets told me that I was lucky to be assigned to his squad. In reality, it wasn't the luck of the draw. He requested me. Johnson had been lost in his own thoughts as was everyone else aboard the chopper. He noticed me looking at him, reached over and placed his hand on my shoulder.

"Nervous, Henry?"

"A little."

"It's okay. I'm just as nervous. No matter how many times you make this trip, you'll still be nervous. You're probably scared, too. But that's okay because as soon as we land and the shit hits the fan, you won't have time to be scared or nervous. Just stick to me like glue and you'll be okay."

"Thanks," I said, feeling a little more secure.

"As soon as your feet hit the ground, run like hell in a zigzag pattern until I tell you to drop. Then hit the ground and hug it until it's time to move out. The Hueys will provide us with fire- cover until everyone is clear of the choppers and they lift off again."

"Don't worry about me," I said with a smile. "I'll stick with you like bonded glue."

Johnson returned my smile, lifted his hand from my shoulder and gave me the thumbs up sign and a reassuring wink. We exchanged nervous smiles.

By now we had been airborne for ten minutes and the sun was clearing the approaching mountain tops. In a few minutes, we would be on the ground at the base of the mountains where the enemy had been reported. The silence in the chopper could be felt over the roaring sounds of the churning blades.

After what seemed like eternity, Lieutenant Smith began to speak. "All right, this is it. Once your feet touch the ground, move out fifty yards and hit the dirt."

While Lieutenant Smith was still issuing instructions, a third of our Huey escorts pulled out in front of the other choppers, increased their speed and headed toward the base of the mountain. When they reached the area where we were scheduled to land, the gunners aboard the gunships opened up with their M-60's, spraying the area with thousands of rounds of machine gun fire.

After laying down a base of fire they pulled back, clearing the way for the choppers carrying the human cargo. The choppers began to descend and another third of the Huey gunships formed a ring around the troop carriers. The Hueys provided us with cover as we jumped off the choppers, screaming at the top of our lungs. The fire power from the gunships was so loud and intense that I couldn't tell if there was any VC or North Vietnamese regulars returning our fire or not.

Within minutes, Bravo and Charlie Company were on the ground. When the last men cleared the choppers, the group of Hueys, which had provided cover for us, pulled away.

The remaining third of the gunships took their positions and provided cover for the troop carriers as they lifted off and sped away.

When all the choppers had flown out of sight, much to our relief, we realized that the landing was a smooth one. We hadn't met any enemy resistance. Charlie (our nickname for the enemy) was smart. He didn't want to tangle with the Hueys. Besides, they had the advantage of knowing exactly where we were for the time being and how many of us there were. On the other hand, we had no idea at all where their positions were, or how many of them were out there waiting for us.

Once it was determined that Charlie wasn't ready to engage us yet, Captain Jenkins called the platoon leaders together and began to lay out the details of the strategy we would use to accomplish our mission. We would pull back a few hundred yards and set up our base of operations. From that point, we would begin our day long searches for the enemy.

It didn't take us long to set up our outpost. First, we dug several trenches for protection, in case of a rocket or mortar attack. Next, we proceeded to set up the command post. Within two hours after we landed, we were ready to start our patrols. The first and second platoons of One-Nine would be the first two to go out on patrol. The route to be taken was carefully planned.

The first platoon would head east and my platoon, the second, would go west. After several clicks, the first platoon would head northwest and mine would travel northeast. If all went well, both platoons would hook-up directly north of our base of operations. We would then make our way back to camp by heading south. We could sweep the entire area in front of our outpost with this tactic. After several such patrols, we would advance farther up the mountains, where a new base of operations would be set up.

This procedure would be repeated until we cleared the mountains and the surrounding area of enemy troops. Once done, we were to hold our position until the Army and ARVN troops arrived. If we were lucky, they would be on schedule, sometime within the next thirty days.

We moved out from camp with the greatest of caution. Although we couldn't be sure where the enemy was waiting for us, we were sure he was. We were also sure that they had set up numerous booby traps to slow us down.

Lance Corporal Bass volunteered to walk point. A Native American, he was born and raised on a reservation somewhere in Arizona. Everyone said he was the best point man in the Corps. He gave full credit for this to his Indian heritage, claiming that Indians had keener senses than the rest of Americans. Like Corporal Johnson, he was a veteran of several previous combat operations and was himself a short-timer. Taking that into account, Lieutenant Smith addressed him. "Listen Bass, you don't have to walk point. You've paid your dues."

"You expect me to depend on one of these rookies to keep us from getting ambushed? I'm too close to going back to the real world to trust anyone else. I'll take point."

Walking point meant walking a good distance ahead of the rest of the platoon. The point man was supposed to be on the lookout for signs of an ambush or booby traps. But it usually wasn't an ambush that got the point man. Charlie was a skilled and tactful fighter. Most of the time, he would let the point man pass and once the main column was in the ambush kill zone, he would open fire. Tripping a booby trap was the point man's biggest worry. Lance Cpl. Bass walked over to where Corporal Johnson and I stood. "You had better watch my ass, Johnson. Keep an eye on baby san here. He promised me an invitation to a party in L. A. next year. I'm looking forward to it."

"You got it. No sweat."

The two of them slapped hands and Bass took his position at point. Lieutenant Smith gave the signal to move out. Within seconds we were on our way.

Although it was still early in the morning, the sun was already beating down on us. So far, our luck was holding out. While the primary objective of our mission was to make contact with the enemy and drive them out of the area, we were just as happy not to have encountered hostile fire after more than two hours of patrol. Our luck had held out for another hour when, suddenly, a familiar sound was heard whistling overhead.

"Incoming!" someone shouted.

Everyone scattered and hit the dirt. The only good thing about a mortar was that you could hear one coming a few seconds before its arrival. In the rear, if you were quick on your feet, you had enough time to make it to a hole. In the bush, the jungle didn't offer much protection. All you could do was flatten your body on the ground and pray that none of the fragments from the exploding rounds had your name on them. As soon as we hit the dirt, several mortars exploded around us. Just as quickly as the shelling began, it stopped. One by one, we popped our heads up from the ground. Lieutenant Smith remained still for a few moments, in anticipation of a renewed mortar attack, then gave the signal. Slowly, we stood up.

"Any casualties?" he asked.

One by one, the squad leaders reported. "First squad all present and accounted for." "Second squad all present and accounted for." "Third squad all present and accounted for." "Fourth squad all present and accounted for."

"Good," responded the Lieutenant. "What about Bass?" he asked as he looked around.

Suddenly it dawned on us that we were all unscratched because the incoming shells had exploded to our rear and front. Johnson tapped my shoulder and said, "Follow me." We ran toward the point as fast as our legs could carry us. Just as we reached a clearing, we saw Bass on the other side. Much to our relief, he gave us the thumbs up sign.

"Cover him," Johnson ordered.

We dropped to the ground and aimed our rifles. Johnson signaled Bass to come across the clearing. I couldn't believe the ease with which he strolled across the opening and joined us.

"Are you okay?" Johnson asked. "I'm fine. Did I worry you?"

"Not for a moment," Johnson responded, as the two hugged and patted each other on the back.

"What's with you, baby san?" Bass asked me, as I knelt there with a dumfounded look on my face. I was still amazed at the manner in which he had strutted across the freshly made clearing. "Are you nuts? Weren't you scared that you might get wasted while you were taking your sweet time across the clearing?" I asked.

"Not for a second. Lesson number one. If Charlie were anywhere near here, he would have saved his mortars and ambushed us instead. He is somewhere just behind those hills over there."

Bass pointed to a small cluster of hills in the distance. "It's our lucky day, for now anyway. If I'm correct, Charlie won't confront us today. He might throw a few more mortars, but he won't greet us in person. Time is on his side. He'll wait us out. The way he sees it, after a week or so of patrolling, we'll get cocky and start to make mistakes. When we do, he'll be waiting to greet us in person."

As Bass finished the first of many lessons he would give me, the rest of the platoon joined up with us, lead by Lieutenant Smith.

"Are you okay Bass?" Lieutenant Smith asked. "I'm fine, sir."

"Glad to hear that. Okay, this is as good a place as any to take a break. We'll rest for fifteen minutes, then head north. We're not going to run into Charlie in person around here."

I looked over at Lance Corporal Bass. He winked, smiled at me, patted me on the shoulder and whispered, "Listen to the Chief, stay close to Johnson, and this will be just like going on a picnic."

He then dropped his pack on the ground, sat, leaned back against it, unsnapped his helmet strap and pulled the helmet down to cover his eyes. Johnson followed suit.

These two have to be the coolest guys under fire one could ever expect to see I thought as I sat and imitated them.

After the break, we continued with our patrol. By late afternoon we met up with the first platoon as scheduled. We learned that they had also come under a mortar attack, but had not been as lucky as us. Three of their men had been wounded. Fortunately, none had been hurt seriously enough to warrant calling in a med-evac chopper. The sight of the three blood-stained bandages covering the wounds of the injured Marines, served as a sharp reminder that suffering and death lurked everywhere in the bush. Lieutenant Bullock, the first platoon leader, had come to the same conclusion as Lieutenant Smith and Bass. Charlie was going to play a waiting game.

It was a few minutes short of twenty hundred hours when we returned to the outpost. We were hungry, exhausted and drenched in sweat.

While on patrol, the outpost had come under an intense rocket and mortar attack. One Marine was killed in the attack and three others suffered wounds that required their immediate evacuation. They were expected to survive if they made it to the hospital alive. After reporting to Captain Jenkins, Lieutenant Smith returned to our platoon area. "The Captain sends his compliments for a job well done."

Job well done, we haven't done a damn thing except hike through the jungle and sweat our asses off all day, were just two of my thoughts.

Almost as if he were reading my mind, the Lieutenant continued to speak. "For many of you, today was your first time out. I know you are probably asking yourself, what did we do? We survived another day in this dirty war and that, in and of itself, is an accomplishment."

Without saying anything else, he turned and walked back toward the command post.

By now, the sun had disappeared, and the temperature had begun its nightly rapid drop. My thoughts of the day's events were interrupted as I heard Johnson's familiar voice. "I don't know about you two but I'm starving. Let's eat."

Without hesitating a second, I got up and followed Johnson and Bass over to a small clearing next to several tree stumps. We opened our cans of C rations and began to eat. I listened to Johnson and Bass as they talked about how Charlie was just messing with us. Both agreed we were lucky Charlie didn't ambush us while we were on patrol. I couldn't help but wonder if we would be as lucky tomorrow as we had been today. In fact, I more than wondered, I prayed that luck would remain on our side.

CHAPTER NINE

During the first week at the outpost, my platoon went on three patrols. Our luck held out. To our individual and collective relief, we failed to make contact with the enemy. Occasionally, the Viet Cong (VC) or North Vietnamese regulars (NVA), we weren't sure, which struck at us from a distance by shelling us with mortars and rockets. To the grunt in the field, it didn't matter which of the two armies was responsible for the shelling. They were both fighting the same war, with the same objective, a free and united Vietnam. In the bush, it made no difference if you were a U.S. Marine, a member of the U.S. Army, Army of the Republic of Vietnam (ARVN), a VC or a NVA regular, once a firefight broke out there was but one goal: to kill the enemy before he killed you.

For some strange reason, it seemed important to the brass back at Third Division Headquarters to know if we were being shelled by the VC or NVA. Contact with the enemy usually meant lives were lost. Yet, the first questions asked upon return from our patrols was always the same; "Did you get a glance at who's out there? Were they VC or NVA regulars?"

Headquarters even went so far as to promise to fly in several cases of ice-cold beer to the first platoon that made contact with the enemy and could identify them as VC or NVA regulars. They must have thought that beer was some type of incentive for us to hope we would run up on the enemy.

Although the outpost came under several heavy rocket and mortar attacks during the past few days, there were only four men wounded. None were seriously injured. The second platoon of Bravo wasn't as lucky as the other platoons in the company. While on patrol, the second day out, they encountered an ambush a few miles west of the outpost. Just as they entered a clearing near the edge of the thick foliage surrounding the mountain all hell broke loose. Caught in a cross fire, they had to scatter. By the time they regrouped, their ambushers had disappeared back into the shelter of the jungle.

When the casualty reports came in, the figures were six Marines killed and fifteen wounded; several seriously. Included among the seriously injured was the platoon leader Lieutenant Bullock. One of the first men killed was the corpsman. After the initial round of gunfire, he didn't hesitate to run to the aid of a wounded comrade who was crying out in pain for help. No sooner had he reached the fallen Marine and begun to comfort him and treat his injuries, than a mortar exploded just feet away, killing him and the other Marine instantly. The radioman was also among the six Marines killed in action. He bought it when a burst of machine gun fire ripped across his body, simultaneously destroying him and the radio. Unable to radio for help, the remainder of the platoon slowly made its way back to the outpost, carrying their dead and wounded. When they approached the camp, men ran to their aid.

"Get a corpsman over here," someone shouted. He could barely be heard above the screams of the wounded.

"Get a med-evac in here," one of the hospital corpsman shouted as he rushed to aid the injured.

I was standing among a group of fellow Marines, watching as the battle-scarred platoon reached the center of the outpost. Captain Jenkins quickly made his way through the crowd and kneeled next to one of the stretchers. I strained to see who was on it. By now, it was almost surrounded by corpsmen and officers.

"How are my men?" asked the injured Marine on the stretcher.

I recognized his voice. It was Lieutenant Bullock. "I let them down."

"You did fine, Lieutenant. You did fine," Captain Jenkins reassured him as he held onto the Lieutenant's hand.

"Choppers are on the way. We'll have you and your men out of here and patched up in no time. Where the hell are those choppers? What's the casualty report?" Captain Jenkins shouted as he stood.

The platoon staff sergeant was just beginning to give Captain Jenkins the casualty figures when one of the corpsmen, who had been attending Lieutenant Bullock called out to the skipper.

"Captain Jenkins, sir."

Captain Jenkins turned his head toward the corpsman just in time to see another corpsman cover the Lieutenant's face with a poncho. The skipper stood there, looking at the Lieutenant's body for a long moment, and then he kicked the dirt, turned away and could be heard muttering, "Shit!"

I knew there were six other Marines killed in the ambush. From where I stood, I could see their bodies lined up and covered with ponchos. Although that sight disturbed me, it didn't upset me as much as seeing Lieutenant Bullock die on the spot. It was the first time I had seen someone die. I stood there in a trance-like state alternating glances between the row of other bodies and Lieutenant Bullock's.

A strange feeling came over me. I wondered if one day soon, some other Marine would stand over me, staring down at my lifeless body. I don't remember how long I stood there, but I do remember a piercing scream that snapped me back into the reality of the moment. Two Marines carrying a stretcher were walking past me. My eyes fell on the injured Marine on the stretcher. I had to cover my mouth to keep from throwing up as they passed. His face had been badly burnt and from the blood-soaked bandages wrapped around his chest and stomach, I concluded that he had been hit several times in the body. Just as they passed, he let out another scream. "Please, somebody help me!" Somehow, I felt I was actually experiencing the same pain he was.

By now, the sounds of the med-evac choppers could be heard as they approached the outpost. A few minutes later, the wounded and dead Marines were placed on the choppers. I stood watching until the last chopper lifted off and disappeared over the hilltops.

When I finally returned to my platoon area, the mood was a somber one. Those of us who had seen for the first-time what war did to the human body would be mentally scared for the rest of our lives. The veterans knew the enemy was through playing a waiting game. They had tasted blood and would be seeking more. I looked at the faces of my comrades, then slowly made my way to where other members of my squad had gathered and flopped down. I closed my eyes and fought back the tears. Suddenly, I felt someone sit down next to me. I kept my eyes closed as I listened to Lance Corporal Bass. "Lesson number two. It's all right to cry. It's when you see this shit and you don't feel like crying that you have to worry. Because if you reach that point, you're already dead. Dead inside." He said no more. He just got up and walked away. I sat there for a long time, trying to forget what I had seen.

I had almost fallen asleep when I heard the whistle go off, signaling a mortar or rocket attack. I sprang up, grabbed my rifle, helmet, flack jacket, a band containing my loaded magazines and dashed for the trench outside the tent. No sooner had I reached the relative safety of the trench, when a round exploded a few feet away.

At first, the rockets could be heard coming in and exploding in groups of two and three. In minutes, they were whistling and exploding all around us at an increased rate. The attack lasted a good hour before there was a lull. We were told to stay in the tunnels and trenches because it wasn't over. Soon, a new barrage of shelling from the enemy broke the silence. There were eleven other Marines in the trench with me. I was relieved when I spied Johnson and Bass at the far end of the trench. I made sure I kept my head below the pile of sandbags that surrounded the top of the trench, as I carefully made my way to where they sat smoking a joint. Johnson spoke first. "You might as well get comfortable, Baby San. We're going to be in here all night. Those are NVA regulars shelling us. They'll keep it up all night, just so that we won't get much rest. They hope that when we patrol tomorrow, we'll be tired and get real sloppy."

"How do you know they're not going to attack tonight?"
"Because they can sit right where they are and fuck with us all night."

"Why doesn't the CO call for an air strike?"

"Because ain't nobody going to fly at night, and Charlie knows it. By time the sun comes up, he'll be underground somewhere, cooling out. You could drop ten tons of shit on them, and you wouldn't scratch a hair on one of their heads," Bass replied in answer to my question.

I decided to take Johnson's advice. I took off my helmet, dropped it onto the ground, removed my flak jacket, placed it against the wall of the trench and leaned against it. It was going to be a long night.

By now, several other guys in the trench had lit up a couple of joints. I declined several offers to take a toke as the shells continued to explode around us. I had just closed my eyes when I heard a voice.

"Want a beer?"

I opened my eyes, shook my head and cracked a smile. "Sure, why not. Where did you get those?" I asked as I reached for the beer being handed me by Private Lopez.

"A friend of mine snuck them in with the supplies that were dropped in this morning. He owed me one. Enjoy! I'm sorry it's not cold."

He then proceeded to hand everyone else in the hole a beer, pausing to take a few tokes along the way.

Lopez was a Puerto Rican from Brooklyn, New York and a supply clerk by MOS. I was told that he had gotten caught making one deal too many back in the rear. He had a choice, join up with a line company, or face a court martial for misappropriation of government property. Considering what he got busted doing, I could not help wondering what other things he had done with the government's property during the seven months he had spent as a supply clerk before joining up with One-Nine. He had been renting portable generators to the local villagers. He called himself the Quang Tri Province Power and Light Company. Everyone knew he was doing it, but nobody cared. Hell, like many things in Vietnam, there were more portable generators around than we needed. He got in trouble when a second lieutenant arrived, fresh from the states, and took over the supply company. Once the lieutenant got wind of Lopez's activities, he wrote him up on charges. So here he was a supply clerk, in the bush with a grunt company. At least he got to spend some time doing what he was originally trained to do. A good number of the black and Hispanic Marines in the bush weren't 0311's either. When they arrived in country, they were simply assigned to combat outfits.

The night seemed to pass ever so slowly, and the pounding of the rockets continued sporadically. After a couple of hours passed, no one in the trench seemed to pay much attention to the ensuing explosions. There hadn't been any reports of casualties and that was uplifting. Between attacks, we stood and looked out over the top of the trench to survey the damage. From what I could see, only a couple of the tents had taken a direct hit. The NVA commanders just wanted to keep us on our toes, so to speak. Bass explained to me that they knew if they did any real damage, the CO would call for artillery fire. All they wanted to do was prevent us from getting a good night's rest. At some point during a lull between shellings, I fell asleep. The light from the early morning sun beaming down on my face awoke me. I looked at my watch. It was barely six a.m. I turned to Bass who was standing up, looking out of the trench.

"Did they stop shelling after I went to sleep?" I asked inquisitively.

"They stopped shelling less than about an hour ago."

"I can't believe I slept through it."

"After awhile, when you're sitting in these stinking holes, you become oblivious to it. If you don't believe me, look around."

I turned my head from side to side. Several of my trench mates were sound asleep. Johnson, along with a few others had already left. I grabbed my gear and climbed out of the trench. I could hear Bass shouting. "Okay, wake up. The party is over."

It felt good to be above ground again. The word was passed that a hot meal was being served in the makeshift mess tent. I washed up and headed over to grab a bite to eat. Johnson and a few other members of my platoon were sitting and eating just outside the tent chowing away. I got a little food and joined them. We were sitting around eating and chatting when word reached us that the Lieutenant wanted to see everyone back at the platoon area. I hastily swallowed a cup of coffee, got up and walked to the barrel of water used to clean our mess kits. I dipped my utensils in the hot water, pulled them back out and shook the water off.

I was one of the last to return to the platoon area. No sooner had I managed to stuff my mess kit in my pack, than Lieutenant Smith and SSgt. Calendar showed up. "Good morning men."

"Good morning," we replied in a reasonable facsimile of harmony.

"I trust everyone slept well last night," Lieutenant Smith continued, somewhat sarcastically.

The one good thing about being in the bush was that all that formal military nonsense, which went on in the rear, was dispensed with. No jumping to attention when an officer entered the tent and stuff like that.

"After yesterday, as many of you well know by now, the party is over. Starting today, we can expect to run up on Charlie at just about every turn. I suggest you get as much rest as you can this morning. The way the CO figures it, and I agree with him, sometime before dusk, Charlie will work his way behind our patrols and set up another ambush or two. We had the luck of the draw. Our platoon has been assigned the task of beating them into position and catching them with their pants down. The first and second squads are the lucky ones. You get to set up the ambush. There is some good news. Headquarters has just informed us that the rest of the battalion and a field artillery unit will join us sometime later this morning. That means we'll increase our patrols and move the outpost in a few days. Enjoy the morning and be ready to pull out at exactly fourteen hundred hours." Lieutenant Smith and SSgt. Calender walked away.

"Fucking ambush!" complained Corporal Mulligan, another combat veteran.

"All we're going to do is lay in the dirt from dusk until dawn for nothing. From those hills, Charlie can keep track of our every move. What a waste of time," Bass commented.

The morning seemed to creep along. Despite having spent the previous night in the trench, most of us weren't sleepy. A little nervous and bored maybe, but not tired. To help pass away the time, a few of the fellows wrote letters. Others just hung around. Johnson, Bass, Lopez and I busied ourselves by playing a game of bid whist. The three of them, along with several others, had just polished off a couple of joints. They claimed that the smoke made their senses keener in the bush. Besides, as Johnson put it. "Ain't shit going to happen out there tonight."

It was around ten thirty when the peace and tranquility was interrupted by the familiar sound of jets streaking overhead. Johnson and Bass dropped their cards and looked to the sky.

I tilted my head in time to see a couple of Phantoms dropping their payload on the mountains and hills in the distance. Parts of the mountains were engulfed in flames. Two by two, a steady stream of F-104's flew overhead and fired their deadly missiles, pounding the terrain and dropping their payloads of napalm. Loud cheers greeted them as they streaked by. They were Marine Corps jets. I recognized the markings, turned to Johnson and commented, "They're a little late, aren't they? Isn't Charlie underground by now?"

"That's just to keep him there until the rest of the battalion arrives. Headquarters doesn't want Charlie firing any rockets, or observing their arrival."

"When will they get here?"

"You should see the choppers rounding the bend any minute now."

Sure enough, no sooner than the words escaped Johnson's mouth, several helicopters could be seen approaching in the distance. Within minutes, dozens of choppers carrying men and equipment, landed, deposited their cargo, then quickly lifted off again. While they unloaded, the jets continued to wreak destruction on the mountains and surrounding hilltops.

The entire landing and equipment drop took slightly more than fifty minutes to complete.

In addition to the rest of the battalion, we were joined by what Lieutenant Smith said would be a small support unit. It looked more like a full support company.

Included in the equipment drop were a half dozen ONTOS with six 106mm recoilless rifles mounted on each, several short-range field artillery pieces and at least a dozen mechanical mules with 106mm recoilless rifles mounted on them. I gazed upon all the equipment and the newly arrived Marines. I didn't need anyone to tell me that someone back at I Corps headquarters expected the area to really heat up in short order. Seeing all that added fire power and additional grunts made me feel a little more secure about being in the middle of nowhere.

Things settled down around one thirty. The battalion CO had arrived and assumed command of the operation from Captain Jenkins. He was a light bird, a Lieutenant Colonel. A veteran of the Korean War, he had been the commander of One-Nine for the past six months. He was a very capable officer who expected a lot from everyone in his command and gave much of himself in return. The first thing he did was call a meeting of all his officers and Staff NCO's. While Lieutenant Smith was at the briefing, we readied our gear.

"Maybe the Colonel will change plans," someone said.

"Fat chance. He probably radioed the orders in himself this morning," Bass replied.

I watched Corporal Johnson as he moved about, checking each of his squad member's gear.

"Tape down those tags," he said to a private, who like myself, was going out on his first ambush.

Do you want to announce to the world that we're out there? Listen up. Make sure your canteens are full and empty your pockets of anything that can make noise. One sound at the wrong moment out there and we're history. As soon as I check your gear, Bass will make sure your faces ain't shining."

Listening and watching Corporal Johnson as he moved among us made me change my first impression of him as a fighter. If he had anything to do with it, we would all return in the same condition we left in.

At exactly fourteen hundred hours, Lieutenant Smith and SSgt. Calendar arrived.

"Is everyone ready?" the Lieutenant asked.

One by one, the squad leaders answered in the affirmative, "Yes sir."

"Good. Now listen carefully. Several patrols will be heading out a few minutes apart. We will split up among them. Once we reach our destination, we will drop out of the column, regroup and set up our ambush. If we break away in that manner and, if we're lucky, Charlie won't even notice. Are there any questions?" Not expecting any, he quickly added, "I want to see the squad leaders outside."

After their briefing, the squad leaders took charge and told us to follow them. We walked to the staging area where we were split into four groups. Each group blended in with one of the platoons about to move out on patrol. It was close to sixteen hundred hours by the time our squads regrouped at the scheduled rendezvous point. We immediately set up an L-shaped ambush. There was little chance of escaping from an "L" shaped ambush. The ambushers would initially position themselves in a straight line, hidden in the bush. Once the intended victims of our ambush walked approximately a third of the way down the line, the tail end of the line of ambushers would swing in at a ninety-degree angle forming the L. Then the trap would be sprung. What you would have at that point, is the victims of the ambush caught in a hail of gunfire from the side and the rear, cutting off their retreat. It was both deadly and extremely effective.

When we were in position and sure our camouflage was effective, we settled in for the long wait. It wouldn't be completely dark for at least five hours, and we had to remain silent and still. The enemy had their scouts out and one movement at the wrong time could alert them to our presence. If that happened, all the waiting would be for nothing.

We were already hot and sweaty when we dug into our position. The sun had been beating down all day and the temperature was at least one hundred-ten degrees. After about two hours, I thought to myself, nothing could be worse. No sooner than I had finished my thought, I discovered the waiting could be made worse. Without warning, the sky opened, and the rain poured down. It was a torrential downpour. In less than a minute, I found myself soaked to the bone. Within seconds the reddish dirt had turned to mud.

In Vietnam, as quickly as the sky opened and soaked the earth, it closed back up and the sun would beat down again, as though it had never taken a break behind the cloud cover. Things had indeed gotten worse. Soaked, hot and absolutely miserable, I now found myself wallowing in a bed of mud. I watched the other members of the squad struggle to get comfortable. I was positioned a few feet away from Johnson. We turned to each other and shook our heads. If Charlie was going to arrive in the area to establish his own ambush, it wouldn't be for a few hours. All we could do was wait and hope he did surface. It disturbed me a little that I actually wished he would show. The thought of my lying in the mud in misery all day, for nothing, didn't please me at all.

The next few hours seemed to drag on endlessly. Finally, the sun began to disappear, and Corporal Johnson gave a silent signal. If Charlie was going to show himself, it would be very soon. We took extreme care not to make a sound, and readied ourselves. Bingo! Our waiting hadn't been in vain. I held my breath as I spied a column of NVA regulars coming down the trail. Their point man had passed our position and hadn't noticed a thing. He signaled the main body that all was clear. I was positioned at the end of our ambush line. My job was to take out the point man.

The column advanced toward our carefully planned surprise party. I trained my sights in on the point man, who by now was a good fifty yards past our trap. He was standing in a clearing, waiting for the rest of his column to continue their advance. Immediately after the column of NVA regulars strolled into the kill zone, the rest of the squad opened fire.

Without hesitation, I squeezed the trigger of my M-16, and sent off a burst of rounds. The first two tore through the point man's head. Several other rounds ripped through his body. I watched, mesmerized, as his lifeless body spun around and dropped to the ground. I had just killed my first man. It left me feeling sick. The screams of the other victims of our ambush snapped me back into the present. I spun around and emptied my magazine into the crowd of NVA soldiers as they scrambled for what little cover, they could find. Methodically, I pulled the empty magazine from my weapon, shoved in a fresh one and continued firing at the enemy. By now, the few NVA who had managed to scurry and crawl into the foliage were returning fire and seeking to escape into the refuge of the jungle. There was little hope for them.

One by one, the would-be escapees were cut down. Most of them fell victim to the rapid and deadly bursts of fire from our two M-60 machine guns. Carefully, we moved out of our concealed positions to check our victims. Lieutenant Smith called for a casualty report. We were lucky only two of our men had been hit. Neither one seriously. Next, we carefully searched the corpses of the NVA regulars.

"Over here," shouted one of the squad members.

Lieutenant Smith and Corporal Johnson ran to the shouting Marine. There were two wounded enemy soldiers trying in vain to play dead.

"Corpsman," the Lieutenant shouted.

Within seconds, the corpsman was kneeling between the two wounded soldiers.

"This one is torn up pretty bad. There isn't shit I can do for him. He'll be dead in a few minutes. This other one, he'll make it."

"See what you can do, Doc."

"What about him?"

Corporal Johnson asked the Lieutenant as he pointed to the mortally wounded NVA regular. Before the Lieutenant could respond to the question, the wounded enemy soldier sucked in a deep breath, then released it as his eyes shut and his head fell to the side.

"Forget him. He's finished."

Johnson stuck his foot out and carefully kicked the NVA soldier, rolling the body over onto its side. The Corpsman walked over and checked the body for signs of life. There were none.

"Search the rest of the bodies for any useful documents," Johnson ordered. "Hines, Ross, give doc a hand with that son of a bitch. We got ourselves a prisoner."

Half-jokingly, Lieutenant Smith added to Johnson's last comment. "Maybe HQ will throw in an extra case of cold beer." A tap on my shoulder startled me. I spun around quickly. It was Bass. "You hit the motherfucker right in the middle of the forehead. Nice work, Henry." He walked away.

I stood there, looking at the carnage; looking at the bloody victims of our successful ambush and listening to Bass telling others in the squad about the clean shot I had put through the head of the point man. I felt sick to my stomach. Sick motherfuckers, I thought, as a couple of the members of my squad passed and slapped me on my shoulder.

"Nice shooting Henry," they said as they passed.

In less than five minutes, we were ready to head back to our temporary base. Hines and Ross fashioned a makeshift stretcher and secured the wounded NVA soldier to it. Doc finished applying a bandage to the shoulder of one of the two wounded Marines. Lieutenant Smith was on the radio to the command bunker. A few of the guys were busy collecting AK- 47's (Russian made rifles) as souvenirs of the battle.

"All right, let's get our asses in tow," SSgt. Calender hollered as the Lieutenant signed off the radio. "If we hang around here any longer, our party just might be spoiled by a few rounds of incoming. Watch your step. Let's move. Henry, pick up the rear. Bass take point."

Bass headed out and the rest of us followed. The P.O.W. was carried past me tied to the stretcher with a gag in his mouth. I could not help notice the frightened look on his face. While I waited for everyone to get a few yards in front of me, I took another long look at the slaughter we were leaving behind. I couldn't help thinking that, instead of a bunch of NVA regulars sprawled out on the ground, that could have just as easily been a bunch of Marines. I snapped my helmet strap closed before we headed back to our base camp. We made it back without further enemy contact. The battalion commander was glad to hear us confirm what everyone seemed to know all along. We were dealing with NVA regulars. He was especially delighted when he found out we had a prisoner.

"Good work, men. A job well-done, Lieutenant."
"Thank you, sir," replied Lieutenant Smith.

"I'll see to it your beer is delivered ASAP. Get a chopper in here at first light. Headquarters will want to talk to our little friend here," the colonel shouted as he turned and walked away.

We returned to our bivouac area. There were no more rookies in the first and second squads. We were all combat veterans now. I was tired, dirty and caked with mud. I paused a moment before cleaning up. All the training had paid off. When it came time to do what I was trained for, I did it without hesitating, and with marked proficiency. I was indeed a highly trained killer. Not that I took pride in that fact, or wanted to brag about it, I just took note of it.

CHAPTER TEN

Near the end of the second week of Operation Cameron Falls, the decision was made to leave the base camp where it was. Someone higher up the chain of command decided that as sitting ducks for rockets, mortars and sniper fire, we could be more effective than if we were doing what Marines were trained to do; engage the enemy directly. We couldn't find the enemy during our constant patrols, yet they found us whenever they wanted. By the middle of the third week, we were under constant bombardment. Our contact with the enemy increased with each new patrol and so did our casualties.

The thing that seemed most important to Division Headquarters back in the rear was that we gave a favorable body-count. Body-count was a somewhat nice way of saying number of enemy killed. A veteran field commander knew how to keep his superiors happy while keeping the heat off him and his unit. If they wanted a sizable body-count back at Division Headquarters, then they got one. We devised a variety of methods of counting bodies. Sometimes we would just make up numbers to report. Other times, we counted fallen trees and dead animals. Another method of arriving at an accurate body- count was to actually count the number of enemy we killed during a firefight, then multiply the number by three or four. The one thing in Vietnam that we could count on was that no big shot from the rear was going to risk getting his ass shot off just to verify the numbers.

Since arriving in country, luck was still on my side. I had been on several patrols and ambushes and hadn't even been scratched, at least physically. Several men in my platoon had gotten wasted and a few others earned an early ticket home. Getting wasted meant being killed in action and getting an early ticket home meant you were shot up so bad that you would require long term medical care back in the states.

The military has a million rules. Few, if any, favored the average combat Marine or soldier. There was one, however, that could work to a fighting man's advantage. If you received three Purple Hearts, you earned an early ticket home. It didn't matter how badly you were hurt. If you were wounded in combat, you were awarded the Purple Heart. After a few days in Vietnam, getting home alive became the main, if not the only objective. With that in mind, men found all sorts of ways to earn the Purple Heart. It wasn't for the monetary value, or any particular prestige attached to the thing. After all, the Purple Heart was made of plastic.

One favorite method to earn an early ticket home was to find a nice piece of shrapnel from an enemy rocket or mortar, and hold on to it. Later, while on patrol, if we came under a rocket or mortar attack, men would push the piece of shrapnel into their arm or leg and call for a corpsman. It got so bad that we were actually searched for shrapnel before going on patrol. Most of the guys who resorted to such underhanded methods were the ones you didn't want in combat with you, anyway.

One of the things that kept you going in the bush was knowing you were with other Marines. You knew the Marines took care of their own. If you were wounded, somehow your fellow Marines would get you out of there. A lot of the men talked about how comforting it was to know that if they were killed in battle, if it was at all possible, their buddies would see to it that their body got home. Personally, that thought never was very comforting.

During the third week of operation Cameron Falls, we received our first mail call in the bush. When it was first announced, everyone's face seemed to light up. By the time the last letter or package had been handed out, the mood was generally a bit more somber than it had been at the start. Each time the mail clerk sounded off a name and someone responded "Dead," it served as a grim reminder that we were at war and in constant danger of becoming "Dead" ourselves.

So far, my own, and the luck of the guys I had befriended in the platoon was holding up. Johnson, Bass and Lopez hadn't so much has been scratched during the past three weeks of frequent fierce battle. That fact made it easier for me to deal with the downside of mailcall. When I heard someone call, "Dead!" to the mail clerk's name calling, I thought about it for a second or two. Then, as if I hadn't heard a thing, I anxiously awaited my name. Mail was often the only thing you had to look forward to in the bush. A nice letter from someone back home could do more to lift spirits and boost morale than anything else. On the other hand, a "Dear John" or other bad news from home could destroy a man's will to survive. After what seemed like forever, I heard my name.

"Henry."

"Yo!" I responded enthusiastically.

I waited anxiously as the letter was passed through the crowd. When the envelope reached me, I knew instantaneously that it wasn't from home. I looked at the return address on the official looking brown envelope. It was from the Department of the Army. Why would I be receiving a thick letter from the Army? I asked myself as I slowly opened the envelope. In my gut, I could feel that something was wrong. My feelings were confirmed the moment I opened it. The cold feeling brown envelope contained the letter I had sent a few weeks earlier to my friend, Fletcher, the Army medic, and a letter from the Army on official stationery.

The tears began to roll down my cheeks as I scanned the letter that read in part; "We regret to inform you that we were unable to deliver your letter. Specialist Fourth Class Fletcher J. Nowlin died on June 3, 1969 from injuries sustained during the battle for Hill 881." I clutched the letter tightly in my hand, swiftly walked away from the crowd, found an isolated area behind the command tent and read the letter again. I thought about the last time that I saw Fletcher. I had also thought about that when I mailed him the letter. At that time, it seemed like I had been back in Queens, New York hanging out with him only a few days earlier. Now it seemed like so long ago. The memories of what a swell person he was were vivid in my mind. The added tragedy was that he hadn't even been fighting. He was a medic, trying to save lives. At that very moment, it didn't seem to matter much when I last saw my friend. The one thing that I knew was that I wouldn't be hanging with him ever again, at least, not back in Queens.

I had clear visions of Fletcher unselfishly running through a hail of gunfire and exploding rockets, to the aid of some injured soldier crying out in pain. "Medic! Medic!" I could see him getting hit and tumbling to the ground. I could see him mortally wounded, crawling on his hands and knees, still trying to reach the injured soldier who had cried out to him. He was that kind of guy. I said a prayer for my friend, inserted the Army's letter, along with my unopened returned one back into the envelope, then carefully folded it and tucked it securely in my pocket. I sat there a few minutes before I wiped my tear stained face and returned to my tent.

In the bush, it was easy to tell when someone had gotten bad news in the mail. I tried hard to hide the fact I had just received that dreaded letter. However, try as I might, my efforts were in vain. I hadn't been back in the tent but a minute or two when Johnson and Bass approached me. Johnson spoke first. "Do you want to talk about it?"

I didn't answer him. Instead, I reached into my pocket and handed him the letter. He and Bass knew all about my friend Fletcher and about how we planned to take R&R together. They read in silence. When they were done, they knew there was nothing they could say that would ease the pain. Johnson simply placed the letter on my air mattress, patted me on my shoulder and walked away. Bass just looked at me with sympathetic eyes. He stood there for a few seconds, at a loss for words. Finally, he laid his hand on my shoulder and spoke in a hushed tone. "I'm sorry, brother. I'm really sorry." Without saying another word, he quickly turned away and followed Johnson outside.

Before I could contemplate too long on the news of Fletcher's death, Johnson and Bass came rushing into the tent. "Let's move. Alpha has run into some shit and we're going to bail them out," Johnson shouted.

Without wasting a second, everyone grabbed his gear and dashed outside. By the time the last man had exited the tent,

Lieutenant Smith and SSgt. Calender arrived. "Listen up, Alpha Company is pinned down in a valley just north of the first cluster of hills. Bravo is going to drop in and give them a hand getting out of there. Remember the LZ (landing zone) is hot as hell." The Lieutenant continued speaking while we were each handed several grenades and additional ammo.

"We're traveling light. We're going in, bail Alpha out and get the hell out of there as quickly as possible. Let's get to the loading zone. Army choppers are flying us in, so let's show them what it means to be Marines."

While we dashed toward the waiting choppers, I caught a glance of a replacement who had arrived the day before. He appeared to be scared to death, just as everyone was his first time out.

"Stick real close to me, Collins, I'll get you back in time for supper," I shouted over the roar of the churning helicopter blades.

Within minutes, we were aboard and on our way to join Alpha Company in battle. Johnson was right when he told me a few weeks earlier that no matter how often you made the trip, you were always nervous. I wasn't as jittery this time because by now I was a veteran fighter. It was a short ride to where the NVA had Alpha Company pinned down. We would be landing roughly two miles in front of Alpha's position and would have to fight our way toward them. This would break up the crossfire that had them pinned down.

Within minutes of takeoff, the choppers were over the LZ. The chopper I was riding in was the first to descend. I turned toward Private Collins. "Remember, when our feet touch the ground, stick close to me and when I say hit the deck, hit it and keep your head down." I hardly had time to finish what I was saying before the chopper was hovering a few feet above the ground. We began jumping out onto the ground, screaming at the top of our lungs as we charged forward. The LZ was indeed hot.

I charged from the chopper, then turned to my left in time to see two Marines get wasted as they emerged from one of the choppers. I raced forward with the rest of the Marines from my company. We were under intense small arms fire from a hidden enemy. Before the last chopper could discharge its load of combatants, the mortars began pouring in. "Incoming! Incoming!," several men shouted.

"Hit the deck," I screamed at Pvt. Collins as I reached out and pulled him to the ground with me.

Suddenly, I heard a loud explosion to my rear. I quickly rolled over to explore the sound. One of the choppers, on which our casualties were being loaded, had taken a direct hit and exploded just as it was attempting to liftoff.

By now we were returning small arms fire. SSgt. Chandler was on the radio calling for artillery. "Fire for effect, no spotters. I repeat, fire for effect," he shouted, after calling off the coordinates.

He then quickly moved away from the radioman. No one wanted to stay too close to him. He was too much of a target, with the radio's whip antenna clearly visible in the distance.

SSgt. Chandler rejoined Captain Jenkins, who was huddled with his officers trying to lay out some strategy. All we could do for the moment was huddle close to the ground, while we waited for our artillery shells to slam into the enemy entrenched in the hills and jungle foliage in front of us. We were exchanging small arms fire with the NVA, with no way of knowing if we were hitting a damn thing. Suddenly, a mortar round exploded to my left. Several Marines screamed. When the smoke cleared, I could see that the round had found its mark. Shrieks of pain pierced my ears.

"Keep low and follow me," I shouted at Collins.

If Collins was still scared, he didn't show it as he followed me to where the injured Marines lay. Bending as low as we could, we hurriedly made our way through a barrage of exploding mortars and small arms fire. Once we reached the fallen Marines' position, it was clear that the mortar had been extremely effective. Fragments from the explosives had killed two of the four Marines. Because of recent casualties, there were many rookies on the operation. All four were cherry boys. They had been huddled too close to each other for their own good. That was a definite no-no during a mortar attack in an open field.

"Corpsman!" I shouted, as I ripped a piece of cloth from the fatigues of one of the injured Marines. His leg was partially torn off just below the knee and a steady stream of blood was gushing out. I reached for my bayonet, to use as part of the tourniquet I was fashioning to apply to the injured Marine. The bodies of the two wasted Marines nearby were almost blown to bits. A few feet away, the second injured Marine sat in shock.

"Get him down," I shouted to Collins, who seemed a little dazed himself. His response was immediate. He quickly pushed the injured Marine to the ground and shielded his body with his own. I returned my attention to the wounded Marine in front of me.

For someone so severely wounded, he was extremely calm. I knew that he had to be experiencing excruciating pain. His resolve not to show his torment amazed me. Just as I finished applying the tourniquet, the whistling sounds of our artillery could be heard overhead. Seconds later, our rounds exploded into the hills and foliage that hid the enemy. After a few dozen rounds had pounded their positions, the shelling stopped from both directions. Our artillery had found its mark. I instructed the Marine, to whom I had just applied the tourniquet, to hold onto it while I checked on his buddy.

"Corpsman! Corpsman" I shouted again.

Cautiously, I crawled over to check on the Marine that Collins had been unselfishly protecting with his body. He had taken a few small fragments from the mortar in the shoulder and thigh. Nothing serious.

"A few stitches, and you'll be as good as new," I assured him.

I knew that he was still in shock and couldn't hear me. I had said what I did more for Collins' benefit. He was obviously a bit shaken up.

"You did fine. See, I told you, stick with me and you'll be okay," I said to Collins in order to set him at ease.

By now the corpsman had made his way to where we were tending to the two wounded Marines.

"What have we here?" he asked, pulling the dazed Marine's hand from over his shoulder wound.

"He is more shocked than anything. His buddy is pretty fucked up though," I whispered to Doc as I pointed to the other injured Marine.

"I did what I could, Doc, but I think his leg is finished," I continued in a hushed tone.

"Thanks, Henry," Doc responded as he turned his attention to the more seriously injured Marine. He checked the injury to the leg first then turned to me. Doc didn't have to say a word, I understood. I was correct in my diagnosis. The Marine's leg was finished.

"Good job, Henry. Thanks!" Doc said, as he pulled out a needle to administer a shot of morphine to the injured Marine who was grimacing in pain as he bit down on a stick Doc had given him.

"Need me for anything else?" I asked.

"Yeah, tell the skipper that if we don't get this man to an aid station real soon, he's a goner," he whispered as he administered the pain killer.

"Let's go, Collins," I blurted in a subdued tone.

When I reached the skipper, he was already on the radio calling for the much needed med-evac choppers. "I need several birds in here ASAP. I got at least a dozen men down and I want them out of here and treated."

"One of the guys is hurt pretty bad sir. Doc thinks were going to lose him if he isn't evacuated quickly."

"Choppers are on the way. I saw what you two did out there. I'm proud of you," the skipper responded as he shook his head and winked at Collins and me.

"Get me a casualty report," he shouted routinely. Gunny was already on his way with the full report.

"The first platoon has three wounded. One seriously. The second platoon has two dead and four wounded. None seriously. The third is unscratched. The fourth platoon is pretty shot up. Four dead and ten wounded including Lieutenant Dunbar. He took a round in the chest. Doc says he'll make it, if we get him out of here ASAP."

I followed Captain Jenkins over to where Lt. Dunbar lay.

"You're going to be all right, son. I'll have you out of here in no time," he assured the Lieutenant, as the sounds of the med- evac choppers were heard in the distance. "I want to see all platoon and squad leaders on the double. Lieutenant Smith, see to the evacuation, then join us."

"Yes, sir," replied Lieutenant Smith before he began issuing instructions. "Henry, grab a few men and help load the wounded."

Within ten minutes, our wounded were loaded on the med- evac choppers and on their way to a hospital ship or a fully equipped aid station. I watched as the choppers disappeared. Vietnam was a strange kind of war. It was truly a mobile one. With lightning speed, they would fly us in and drop us off in the middle of a hot landing zone. Then, just as quickly, they would return and fly the dead and wounded back to the rear.

It was somewhat ironic that, if you were unfortunate enough to get wounded, you would be better off getting wounded in the bush than back at the combat base. The injuries that were sustained at the combat base usually occurred during rocket and mortar attacks. More often than not, the incoming fire was so intense that it was far too risky for choppers to fly in and out of the base during the attack. So if you were wounded in the attack, you were dependent on the skills of a corpsman, until the assault stopped and you could be carried to the aid station or, if the injures sustained were serious enough, a chopper could get in to carry you out.

A total of thirty-five minutes passed since we first hit the LZ. There hadn't been any more mortars lobbed or small arms rounds fired at us since our artillery pounded the hills to our immediate front. We could still hear the sounds of battle in the distance. It sounded like Alpha was indeed having a rough go of it.

After their briefing, the surviving platoon members and squad leaders returned to where their company had gather. Lieutenant Smith addressed us. "Lieutenant Dunbar and the 4th platoon's assist platoon leader, Sgt. Lawrence were hit pretty bad. Both had to be evacuated. SSgt. Calender has temporarily been assigned as the 4th platoon leader. Corporal Johnson, you're now second in command of the 3rd platoon. Henry, the first squad is yours. We're moving out in five minutes. We have to cross through that jungle up ahead to get to Alpha. You can expect Charlie to be waiting for us. Keep alert and watch your step. Bass, the point is yours. Be careful."

"You bet, sir."

Corporal Johnson walked over to me and spoke. "Take care of the rookies, Henry, and watch your ass."

"No sweat," I replied, with a sense of renewed confidence.

A few minutes later, we were trudging forward. We reached the edge of the jungle without encountering any further resistance from the enemy. Apparently, our artillery had been effective. The jungle foliage was thick, except in spots where the artillery had blown it away, or the napalm from our jets had burned it off earlier that day.

121

We moved at a snail's pace literally cutting a path as we went. My squad was in the lead. I felt a tremendous amount of responsibility in my new position as squad leader. Except for six other men, who joined the squad at the same time I did, it was made up of rookies who were experiencing combat for the first time. We had gone a few hundred yards into the thick, green jungle, when suddenly Bass signaled for the column to halt. I stopped dead in my tracks and passed the signal back. Bass then waved me forward. I ordered my squad to stay put, then carefully made my way to Bass. When I reached him, he was smiling, "Clever little bastards, they are. Watch this," he said.

Cautiously, he pushed aside a pile of leaves with the tip of his boot. Beneath was a thin piece of wire stretched across the narrow jungle path.

"Step over here," Bass continued. He moved to the side, then carefully sprawled out flat on the ground. "You had better get your ass down if you want to keep it in one piece." Without a moment's hesitation, I joined him.

"Check this out," Bass said, while calculatedly extending his arm and pulling the wire. I jerked my neck up slightly in response to a swishing sound, a few feet above where we lay. My mouth dropped open as I saw a large board full of spikes sweep down out of one tree and slam into the trunk of another one immediately to our rear.

"It was set at just about the right height to rip through someone's chest and cut them in half," Bass informed me as he got up. I followed suit and walked over to the booby trap embedded in the tree to examine it at close range. The thought of such a simple yet deadly device slamming into my chest sent shudders throughout my entire body.

"Show's over. Back to your squad. Alpha's waiting."

I hastily made my way back to my squad. By then, Lieutenant Smith had made his way up to the front of the column. "What's the hold up?" he inquired.

"Booby trap. It's clear now," I answered. "Good, let's get this show on the road."

Lieutenant Smith returned to the middle of the column. We moved out again. The battle between Alpha and the NVA grew louder with each step. They were somewhere on the other side of the thick bush we had been so guardedly making our way through. Suddenly, the NVA who obviously had been expecting us opened fire. We hit the deck and returned fire. One of my squad members was hit in the opening burst of enemy fire. "Are you okay Webber?" I asked.

"I took one in the leg. Nothing to sweat. I'll make it." "Can you make it back to Doc?"

"I'll try," Private Webber answered.

Captain Jenkins and Lt. Smith quickly made their way to the front of the column. "Where's Bass?" the Lieutenant inquired.

I had momentarily forgotten about him. Much to my relief, just as I looked in the direction, I had last seen him. He gave us the thumbs up sign.

"Get those 60's up here," Captain Jenkins shouted over his shoulder. The hail of small arms fire from the NVA had us pinned down for the moment. "Well, at least we're taking some of the heat off Alpha," he commented.

The machine gunners and their partners reached our position a few seconds later. Captain Jenkins immediately began issuing orders. "I want a continuous line of fire right along that treeline to the left. Henry, when I tell you, move your squad out to the edge of the clearing, then position yourself to cover our advance."

"Yes, sir," I responded to Captain Jenkins clear and precise orders.

"Lieutenant, bring up the rest of your platoon and cover the first squad."

"Yes sir," replied Lieutenant Smith, as he signaled for the rest of the platoon to make their way to where we lay.

The machine gunners opened up, spraying the tree line, covering the rest of the platoon's advance. Once they joined us, the Captain gave the command, "Hit it!"

With the two machine gunners and the rest of the platoon providing an awesome display of small arms fire for cover, I signaled my squad to move out. We leaped to our feet and charged forward screaming at the top of our young lungs. We passed Bass, who jumped up and joined us in our charge. We ran as fast as our legs could carry us, still screaming and firing our rifles into the jungle to our left and right. It seemed to take forever to reach the edge of the clearing. Finally, we reached it and dropped to the ground. I heard one of my men screaming. "I'm hit! I'm hit!"

I turned around in time to see him falling to the ground. "Watch my ass," I shouted to Bass and Collins before springing up and running to the aid of my injured squad member. "Where are you hit, Diorio?"

"In my left leg."

"Well let's get ready to do the bunny hop," I joked. Then I threw his arm around my neck, wrapped my arm around his waist and helped him stand. We were no sooner on our feet, when I heard Bass shout. "Incoming!"

Instinctively, I dropped to the ground, pulling Diorio with me. He let out a shrill as he fell on his injured leg. Several mortars exploded around us. "It's now or never, Diorio. If we stay here any longer, we're going to get wasted for sure. I'll carry you. Hold my rifle."

Diorio took my M-16 as I slid around and positioned myself so I could throw him over my shoulders. "Ready?"

"As ready as I'll ever be," was his nervous response. I stood quickly, pulled Pfc. Diorio up with me, bent slightly and threw him across my shoulders in a deadman's carry. It was obvious that the machine gunners saw what was going on because they began concentrating their fire power in the direction where the mortars were most likely coming from. Bass and the rest of my squad were laying down a heavy line of fire at the tree lines to the left and right. I prayed for a safe deliverance as I dashed through a barrage of gunfire and exploding mortars. When I reached the relative safety of my squad, I dropped to the ground so hastily that I grimaced from the pain that shot through my thighs when my knees slammed onto the ground. I fell backward, and released my hold on Diorio and let out a deep breath.

"Thanks, Henry, I owe you one."

"Forget it," I replied, before turning my attention to the battle at hand.

"The heaviest fire is coming from behind that cluster of trees over there," Bass informed me.

I signaled to the Lieutenant, letting him know where to concentrate the machine gun fire. In response, he and the rest of the platoon began their forward advance. Squad by squad, the remainder of the platoon charged through the jungle under a sporadic barrage of mortar and small arms fire. Our artillery fire had been more effective than we had anticipated.

Collectively, the bullets from our M-60's and the small arms fire we showered on the enemy from our forward position provided a pretty good shield for the advance. It took less than five minutes for the entire company to reach the edge of the clearing. From where we were positioned, we could see the embattled men of Alpha Company. They were a few hundred yards away, on the other side of another clearing, just inside the treeline.

Later, we would learn that Alpha's radioman had been hit immediately after he radioed in that they were pinned down in crossfire. The radio was damaged and, therefore, they hadn't been able to call in the coordinates for close air or artillery support. Captain Jenkins surveyed the area, then called in the coordinates for a close air attack. While he waited for the jets to arrive and deliver their deadly payload, he briefed the platoon leaders. "After the air strike, Lieutenant Smith, you'll take command of the first and second platoons and mop up the left flank. I'll move across the clearing with the rest of the company and link up with Alpha. Once you've sent Charlie packing, set up a perimeter around the clearing and signal me with a flare. Henry, you and your squad will stay here with the radioman. Once you see the flare, radio in for our ride out. Keep an eye out for back door visitors."

Within minutes, several Phantom jets streaked over our position and, with pinpoint accuracy delivered their payload on the enemy positions to the rear of Alpha Company. We watched the jungle become engulfed in flames where the bombs made contact with mother earth. What little wind there was blew in our direction and carried the distinct stench of burning flesh and napalm. Without waiting for the flames to die down or for the smoke to clear, Captain Jenkins gave the command. "Move out!"

The scene of my fellow Marines jumping to their feet and charging forward, screaming and firing their weapons, reminded me of the scenes from old western flicks. Alpha was pinned down like the wagon trains surrounded by Indians in the movies, while the fearless, heroic cavalry dashed to their rescue. I watched with mixed feelings as I saw several Marines of the third and fourth platoons get cut down. "Collins, Wilson, Ross, get them back here," I shouted. Like true Marines, without hesitation or regard for their own safety, the three of them sprang up and dashed to the rescue of their fallen comrades.

By now, it was obvious that our combined efforts were too much for the enemy. The close air attack had silenced their mortars and rockets. Lt. Smith had met with only a minimum of resistance from small arms fire. Except for three Marines who were hit during the first few seconds of the charge, the rest of the company appeared to make it safely to the tree line on the other side of the clearing. Judging by the movement of the Marines in front of us, the enemy was on the run. Instead of digging in next to Alpha Company, the men of Bravo Company continued to charge a few hundred feet into the jungle. When I saw the purple smoke from the flare, I gave the radioman our coordinates and instructed him, "Call it in."

It didn't take the NVA very long to disappear deep into the jungle. We had forced them to retreat. After four years of battling each other, our enemy got to know us and we got to know them. They knew choppers would arrive in a few minutes to carry us out. Once they landed and we began running to board them, they would again lob mortars at us from their newly concealed position.

Since my squad was covering the rear flank, we would be the last to board the choppers. It took them around fifteen minutes to begin arriving. No sooner had the first group landed, than mortars began arriving again. Since the main purpose of the mission was to bail Alpha out of their jam, they were the first to board the choppers.

The weary and exhausted men of Alpha Company dashed for the waiting choppers seemingly oblivious to the mortar shells exploding around them. The first group was lucky. They managed to board without sustaining additional injuries. Once the choppers were safely out of the area, Captain Jenkins decided to call for another air strike, to be followed by a battery of artillery fire before any more choppers came in. There was no point risking the loss of more men or choppers.

Twenty minutes later, the air strike was over. When our artillery ceased pounding the jungle in front of us, the choppers flew back in and, in short order, we were headed back to our base camp. It had been a long day. Once again, the Walking Dead had been put to the test and, once again, the men of the battalion had distinguished themselves in battle.

I spent the next thirty minutes or so cleaning my gear and myself, then returned to my tent, and pulled out the letter I had received earlier in the day. The call to battle had prevented me from mourning my dead friend. I was deeply hurt and upset by the news of Fletcher's death and recalled the scene a few hours earlier of the wounded and dead men of Alpha Company being loaded onto the choppers. I thought about Fletcher and about the men killed in battle earlier that day. They had relatives and friends who would soon receive news of their deaths. They too would hurt and mourn their loved ones, just as I mourned Fletcher's death.

This was the first time that I really had taken time to think about the people who suffered during a war. It wasn't just the fighters on both sides. There were hundreds of thousands of North and South Vietnamese civilians killed and injured during the years of fighting. Others had suffered as they saw their homes and way of life destroyed. Still others suffered when they received word that their sons, husbands, fathers, brothers and friends had died in battle. I thought about the Viet Cong and the North Vietnamese Regulars, who had just been killed in battle. Were they less human than our allies or we? Of course not! They felt pain and suffered just as we did. The families of their dead and wounded suffered and mourned for them, just as ours did for us.

As my thoughts grew deeper, I realized that if I let thoughts about the reality of war continue to flow through my mind, I would become severely depressed. I folded the letter, stuffed it back into my pocket, then stretched out on my cot and closed my eyes. I desperately wanted to lose myself to sleep and the temporary relief it brought from the pain of war. Physically tired and emotionally drained, I closed my eyes.

CHAPTER ELEVEN

At the end of the fourth week, Division pulled the plug on our base camp. Operation Cameron Falls had officially ended. Elements of the U.S. Army and the Army of the Republic of Vietnam had arrived right on schedule.

Compared to previous casualty rates suffered by the Walking Dead, the overall casualty rate suffered by the battalion during operation Cameron Falls was considered to be light. Enemy contact was also considered to have been light. Division Headquarters attributed our infrequent contact with the enemy to the success of the 9th Marine Regiment's previous thrusts into the area. Such reasoning made for a good report to the press and I Corps Command. Those of us who were in the thick of the shit knew better.

During Operation Cameron Falls, we accounted for 110 enemy soldiers killed and over 1000 weapons of various types captured. There seemed to be one important question that no one back at headquarters bothered to ask. "One hundred and ten enemy soldiers killed out of how many?"

When Division reported that our contact with the enemy was light, it meant that it wasn't frequent. When we did make contact, it was anything but light. Judging by the ferocity of the firefights we had engaged in over the past month, it didn't require much brain power to figure out that there was a large enemy force out there during the entire operation. For whatever reason, they chose not to throw everything they had at us at once.

When we returned to Vandergrift Combat Base, we were told of the success of the rest of the 9th Marines. They had been involved in a joint search and clear operation in the area of the old Khe Sanh Combat Base. By now, I automatically questioned the use of the word "success."

After seeing firsthand how body counts were conducted, I had to laugh at the reports of the number of enemy soldiers killed during an operation. If anyone in authority ever bothered to analyze the reports, they would have to draw one of two conclusions. Either the number of enemy soldiers was far greater than intelligence ever reported, or someone was out and out lying. But the large numbers seemed to make some people happy because we were always congratulated for killing so many enemy soldiers and rewarded with case after case of beer.

Personally, our return to Vandergrift, after participating in Cameron Falls, was a time of joy and sadness. Joyous because the day after we returned, Corporal Johnson was scheduled to rotate back to the real world. I felt good for him. He had spent his time in hell and it was his turn to return to the real world. Not only had he made it through, but he was also credited with helping many others survive Vietnam. The night before he climbed aboard the chopper to leave, we gave him one hell of a party. Johnson was, without a doubt, one of the most popular Marines ever to serve with the Walking Dead. Somewhere around halfway through the party, he pulled me aside and, for the first time, showed signs of fear. "Well, Henry, one more day and a wakeup. Tomorrow this shit will all be over for me. By this time next week, all this shit will seem like it was nothing but a bad dream."

"You know it. I hope we can get together when I get back next year," I responded a bit enviously but extremely happy for him.

"That's just it. I just spent a year caught up in this shit, just thinking about getting home. Now I'm going home, and I haven't the foggiest idea of what I'm going to do when I get there. That scares me. Do you ever think about what you're going to do when you get home?"

I thought about Johnson's question for a few moments before answering. "Come to think of it, I haven't given any thought to it, either."

"Funny thing is, Henry, when the Judge gave me the choice of either going to the joint or joining the Marines, I figured that the Marines would give me the opportunity to learn a trade and give me time to think about my future. Some trade! I wonder what the job market is like back home for a trained killer. All I've had time to think about was this goddamned war and staying alive. One thing has been cleared up in my mind, you can't trust whitey. I've seen him pull some funky shit over here. When you're here a while longer, you'll see what I'm talking about."

I listened attentively to the words of an angry black man. "I'll get home and some whitey will cut his eyes at me or look down at me just because I'm black and call me a nigger behind my back. It ain't no different over here than it is back home. In the bush, we all need each other for survival, but in the rear it's like we're dirt. Where are the black officers? Where are the black pilots? A whole year over here and the only brothers I've run into were putting their lives on the

132

line out in the bush. There was a black lieutenant in Delta Company a few months back. He got an early ticket home in a body bag. Rumor had it that some white boy radioman, who didn't think the brother was qualified to read a map, changed the coordinates the Lieutenant had given him to radio in for air support. Next thing anyone knew a ton of shit was dropped right on their own position."

Johnson paused for a few seconds to collect his thoughts before continuing, "Quiet as it's kept, Henry, I'm mad as hell. Sometimes I think I should have gone to jail instead of going through this shit. I'll probably wind up in jail anyway, because if some whitey crosses me back in the states, I know I'll make a ghost of him without so much as blinking an eye. Listen to me carefully. Don't make the mistake I did over here. Each day when you get up, after you thank the Lord for still being alive, think about what you're going to do when you get home. Make plans, brother, make plans."

I wanted desperately to say something that would offer comfort and ease the hurt I sensed Johnson was feeling. Temporarily lost for words, I just stared at him. We both knew that there was nothing I could say.

"So what the fuck are we standing around getting depressed about. The party's for me, so let's party!" Johnson shouted. His mood appeared to make a 180 degree turn.

We celebrated throughout the night. Before anyone realized it, the night was over and the sun was making its grand entrance, ushering in a new day. I stood outside the hooch looking up at the peaceful sunrise. It suddenly occurred to me that not once during the night did I hear the all too familiar sounds of the war. There were no mortar or rocket attacks, no whistling of artillery shells passing overhead, not even the crackling sound of small arms fire in the distance. That struck me as strange. Not a day or night had gone by since my arrival in country, that I hadn't heard those sounds, at least somewhere in the distance, echoing throughout the night.

A creepy feeling came over me. I listened to the silence and watched the huge fireball begin to brighten up an otherwise dull landscape. The peace and serenity was unnatural and almost frightening. I had the feeling that at any moment something terrible was going to happen. I began to imagine all sorts of possibilities. Perhaps at any moment, a hail of rockets would drop down on us. Maybe tens of thousands of North Vietnamese would suddenly come storming down from the hills and overrun our base.

It was Sunday morning and, even after what happened at Pearl Harbor, the military seemed to drop its guard on Sundays. We didn't run many patrols on Sundays. At least not out of our combat base. However, if you were unfortunate enough to be humping in the bush, the war didn't stop. I knew that I wasn't psychic or anything, but deep down in my gut, I could feel that something was amiss. Before I could dwell on my feeling, the sudden and unexpected sounds of a human voice almost caused me to jump clear out of my pants. "Morning, little brother."

I turned around quickly while simultaneously reached for my forty-five. By the time I spun around, Bass was bent over with laughter. I must have made a funny sight reaching for my forty- five like I was a Marshall Dillon or Paladin. If I really needed to draw it for protection, I would have been dead as a door nail because the damn thing was snug in the holster with the flap snapped shut. Besides that, there wasn't even a round in the chamber.

"You scared the shit out of me," I responded, regaining my composure.

I was known around the battalion for my keen sense of hearing. No one could sneak up on me without my detecting them. That is, no one except Bass. That's why he made such an excellent point man. He could move about unheard, even while carrying a full load of combat gear.

"You're slipping," Bass delighted in saying as he wound down his laughter.

"It's going to be one hell of a hot day," I announced.

"What are you talking about? It's always hot over here, or haven't you noticed?"

He was, of course, right. Even when an occasional breeze made its way through the area, it did very little to ease the sizzling heat. It only got worse after one of the many sudden torrential downpours because then you were both hot and wet.

Although the intensity of the heat dried your fatigues quickly enough, for the short while you were wet, it was sheer misery.

"Ten more days, and it will be me leaving this living hell." "Ten more months, and it will be me leaving this dump," I replied half-jokingly. "Where's brother Johnson?" I continued. "He's packing his shit. He'll be out in a minute," Bass cheerfully answered.

"I'm going to miss him, but I'm glad he's getting out of here in one piece."

"Me too. But not for long, because I'm right on his ass."

"I hear you," I responded.

Before we could continue our light conversation, a beaming Johnson emerged from the tent, carrying his sea bag and a large gym bag. He dropped them onto the ground, placed both his hands on his chest and began rubbing up and down as he took in a deep breath of the early morning air. "Ah, what a beautiful day. Smell the fresh clean air. Feel the warm rays from the sun," he said, somewhat sarcastically as he surveyed the area.

"You can keep this shit. By tomorrow, I'll be breathing in good old American air. Let's go chow down."

"What time is your ride out of here?" I asked.

"I'm scheduled to fly out of here at eight hundred hours. No, make that eight a.m., if you get my drift."

We shared a laugh. I reached down and picked up Johnson's sea bag while Bass picked up his gym bag.

"Well, what are we standing around here for. I know you're dying for your last taste of bush food," I said.

Bass and I draped an arm over Johnson's shoulders and headed toward the mess tent. We were greeted at the entrance by the mess sergeant. He was a lifer and a giant of a Marine. His large six-foot six frame seemed to dwarf us as he spoke. "Well, if it ain't frick, frack and fromp. You're a little early. But knowing how much you will miss my cooking in a day or two, I'll make an exception."

He stepped inside the mess tent and with a sweeping motion of his hand, ushered us in. This was his second tour in Vietnam. He was a native of New Jersey and fond of all his home boys. To him, if you were black and from a large city, you were a home boy. So just about all the black Marines were his home boys.

Almost no one admitted being from a small town or from out in the country. Everyone identified with a big city or found ways to avoid clearly identifying where they were from if it was a small town. Most of the guys from Louisiana or Alabama would say they were from LA. It was sort of funny because when they said that, you knew they weren't talking about Los Angeles. You could tell by their drawl or accent that the L.A. stood for Louisiana, Lower Alabama or Little Rock, Arkansas. Once we were seated, SSgt. Anderson joined us at our table. "What'll you have Johnson? Forget what's on the menu. For your last meal here, I'll whip up whatever you want. The same for your two sidekicks."

"How about some French toast and bacon?"

"You got it. What about you two?" the sergeant inquired. "I'll have the same," I answered hastily.

"Sounds good to me," Bass chimed in.

SSgt. Anderson excused himself and went into the kitchen. "No more Marine Corps food. The first thing I'm going to do, when I get back to the real world, is treat myself to a steak dinner at the finest restaurant on the coast. I'm going to pig out."

"I hear that!" was my response.

"Well, when you get there, don't sit there eating too long. If you do, you might look up and see me seated next to you joining you," Bass added.

It wasn't long before SSgt. Anderson reappeared carrying our food on a tray. He had a white towel draped across his arm and was wearing a crisp white chef's hat.

"Your order, gentlemen. And I do use the term 'gentlemen' lightly."

He placed our food in front of us and continued to carry on as if we were in one of the world's finer restaurants and we were getting the kind of first-class service that people paid for in such establishments. When he was finished serving us, he patted Johnson on the shoulder. "You take care of yourself brother. Just remember this. You got through this shit in one piece. Ain't nothing in the real world compared to this shit. You make something of yourself."

Before Johnson could answer, SSgt. Anderson walked away and disappeared into the kitchen.

We were just finishing our meal when the mess tent officially opened for breakfast. All the black Marines and a handful of others made it a point to stop by our table and wish Johnson good luck on their way to the chow line. When we were through eating breakfast, it seemed to take forever to get from where we were seated to the trash can. Johnson stopped at almost every table and shook the extended hands of his well-wishers. It took him a little longer to shake the brothers' hands than the white Marines. The black handshake, Vietnam style, took a good ten seconds to complete.

There were several versions of the black handshake. At times, that could be very confusing to the persons attempting to execute it, to say nothing of how confusing it appeared to an onlooker. It was just our way of showing that we were somehow part of the Black Power Movement that was growing back in the states. It must have been a threat to the stability of the Marine Corps, because an order was eventually issued by some bozo in the rear banning us from shaking hands in any manner other than the traditional American handshake.

It was okay for some white Marines to hang Confederate flags in the tents and do the Nixon with two fingers, but the black handshake was a threat to racial harmony. The order wasn't enforced too long. The commanders in the field knew that trying to enforce it would only add fuel to the already precarious racial situation. Occasionally, some second lieutenant, fresh out of OCS would arrive and try to enforce the order. He usually paid for his folly.

Finally, we were out of the tent. I looked at my watch. It was seven-forty. The helicopter that will take Johnson to freedom should be arriving momentarily, I thought, just before turning to Johnson. "You tell your mother how much I appreciated all those packages of goodies."

One of the greatest pleasures in Vietnam was tearing into a package from home. Most of the time, we shared the goodies with our buddies. Once a month, like clockwork, Johnson's mother sent a huge package of home baked chocolate chip cookies and other porgy bait (junk food). "I think I'll miss your mom's cookies more than I'll miss you," Bass jokingly said.

"Probably," Johnson answered with a smile.

Before we could continue with our small talk, the distinctive sound of a chopper was heard. The three of us looked at each other wordlessly as we eyed the approaching chopper, making its way around the mountains. In a short time, Bass and I would be saying good-bye to a good friend.

The next few minutes were awkward for the three of us. We stood in silence, watching the chopper approach the landing zone, then gently set down. We were at a loss for words. We knew that we would miss, Johnson and he would miss us.

America is a great country for learning, except when it comes to things like how to express your feelings if you are a man. After the chopper shut its engines, we strolled toward it. Halfway there, we stopped dead in our tracks. An officer climbed out of the chopper, carrying his sea bag and another bag.

"I'll be damned! Are my eyes deceiving me or is that a black first lieutenant or what!" exclaimed Johnson.

"He's black for sure," I replied.

When the newly arrived lieutenant reached us, we snapped to attention and saluted him with vigor and renewed pride.

"Good morning, men," he returned our salute, winked and gave us a quick nod as he passed.

Our facial expressions didn't hide the fact we were glad to see him.

"You guys had better look out for him. Don't let one of those rednecks shoot him in the back," Johnson instructed.

"Ain't nothing going to happen to him, I promise you that.

You know SSgt. Calender will take good care of him."

The morning was full of surprises. The initial shock of seeing our first black first lieutenant in the bush had barely taken hold when we were hit with an even bigger shock. Our mouths dropped wide open as the pilot of the chopper emerged. He was a black captain. We raised our arms to salute him, but he waved it off.

"What's happening, bloods?" he asked. Most of the chopper pilots were relaxed and didn't stand on formalities. They were a unique breed.

"Which one of you is the lucky guy I'm ferrying out of here?" "I am, sir," Johnson replied, in a voice beaming with joy. "Well, hop aboard. I'm going to grab a cup of coffee. I'll be back in a few minutes."

The captain proceeded toward the mess tent. Johnson, Bass, and I looked at one another, then slapped each other five.

"Ain't that a bitch, two black officers in one day. I wouldn't believe it if I didn't see it with my own two eyes. If one of you wrote me and told me about it, I wouldn't believe you. Maybe the Corps is trying to clean up its act."

"I doubt it," was my response to Johnson's remark. "I'll tell you what, I'll keep track of the number of black officers I run across during the next few months. I'm willing to bet you that I won't see a dozen all together."

"That would be a sucker's bet, Henry. Both you and I know you would win hands down."

When we reached the helicopter, we threw Johnson's bags inside. He was about to climb aboard when a group of the guys from the company, led by Captain Jenkins and Lieutenant Smith, caught up with us. We were about to salute when Captain Jenkins spoke. "Forget the salute. I just wanted to let you know that it was a pleasure and a privilege to have had you in my command, Corporal Johnson."

"The same goes for me," added the lieutenant.

"The men and I chipped in and bought you this camera. It's just our way of saying thanks. A lot of good men owe their lives to your skill and dedication. Make sure that you send us a few pictures from home."

Captain Jenkins extended his hand. He and Johnson exchanged a hearty handshake. Lieutenant Smith and the rest of the men followed suit. By the time they were finished, the pilot had returned to his chopper.

"All aboard that's going aboard," he shouted from the cockpit as he revved up the chopper's engines.

Bass shook Johnson's hand and stepped away, while Johnson and I stood in silence for a few seconds, then embraced each other.

"You take care of yourself, little brother. I'll kick your ass when I see you again, if you so much as scratch yourself."

"I'll see you in a few months," I quipped as we broke our embrace.

"Get the fuck out of here," I shouted affectionately over the roar of the churning chopper blades.

We stepped away from the landing zone as Johnson climbed aboard. The pilot had signaled that he was about to take off when I spied one of the Vietnamese, who worked on the base doing laundry and other odd jobs, shouting Johnson's name and running toward the chopper from the far side. No one paid any attention to him. From where I stood, I could see that he was clutching something tightly in his hand. I assumed that he had a present of some sort for Johnson because Johnson was always friendly toward the Vietnamese who worked on or hung around the base.

The pilot didn't see the villager. He was barely off the ground when the villager ducked under the chopper and threw the object he had been carrying into the open door.

The pilot had continued his lift off when suddenly we heard an explosion from inside. In a fraction of a second, the entire chopper blew apart, shooting spinning chunks of metal in every direction. Everyone standing in the distance watching Johnson's departure hit the dirt. Everyone except me. I stood frozen, in a state of shock.

It was nothing short of a miracle that kept me from being cut down by pieces of shrapnel. I saw the Vietnamese, who had thrown the explosive device, running as fast as his legs could carry him. Without hesitating, I reached down and snatched an M-16 off the ground that another Marine dropped when he dove for cover. I aimed at the fleeing saboteur and squeezed the trigger. Several rounds tore into him in rapid succession, throwing him forward a few feet before he fell to the ground. I dropped the rifle and ran to where he had fallen. I didn't know if he was dead or alive. I didn't care. When I reached him, I stood there a few seconds before I removed my forty-five from its holster. I looked down at the gaping holes the M-16 rounds had made in his body.

"You motherfucker!" I shouted before proceeding to empty the rounds from my pistol into the already lifeless body. "You bastard!" I continued to shout.

I pulled the empty magazine from the butt of the pistol and inserted a fully loaded clip. Before I could slide a new round into the chamber, someone grabbed me from behind.

"He's finished, Henry, he's finished."

I recognized the voice. It was Bass. I turned around. We looked at each other in silence, then I glanced back at the burning wreckage. Neither of us made any attempt to hold back the tears. To this day, I have never felt anything close to the hurt and the pain I felt at that moment.

The next several days were a few of the most depressing of my life. Tensions were very high around the base, especially among the black Marines. We were angered and hurt by what had happened to Johnson. All the white Marines knew how angry we were because for several days after Johnson's tragic death, they stayed clear of us. Even the hardened rednecks dared not throw a dirty look at a black Marine, or make any racial slurs. For the first time since my arrival in Vietnam, there seemed to be a peaceful coexistence between the black and white Marines, however artificial it may have been.

The base came under constant shelling that Thursday and Friday. We increased our patrols around the base and several artillery units pounded the surrounding hills with countless shells. By late Saturday, the North Vietnamese had enough and discontinued their shelling. They knew if they stopped, we would in turn, stop shelling them. That seemed to be the way the whole war was fought. They controlled the fighting between ground units, and they controlled the artillery battles. In fact, the entire pace of the war seemed to be under their control, despite what the news media was reporting back home. The shelling, although intense at times, didn't cause any real damage. A couple of Marines, who were slow in getting to the safety of the trenches, suffered minor wounds.

It was on Sunday evening, one week to the day after Johnson's death, that all hell broke loose at Vandergrift Combat Base. Earlier in the day, the word was passed around that a movie was to be shown at the makeshift theater, put up on the field where the choppers landed.

It was a typical lazy Sunday and, by the time dusk set in, we were all looking forward to our treat. We had no way of knowing what the movie would be. The helicopter carrying the film had arrived a few minutes earlier and the sergeant in charge of the film wouldn't tell anyone the title. He wanted it to be a surprise. Well, that turned out to be a grave error. Had he disclosed it, he would have known immediately from the general feedback, that it wouldn't have been a good idea to show it.

The film was scheduled to start just after dark, around nine- thirty. By the time the sun had disappeared completely over the horizon, a good number of the Marines were high on a variety of substances. Some on pot, some on acid, some on beer and a few others on God only knew what. So there sat several hundred high, tired, angry and frustrated Marines, huddled around the makeshift screen, waiting for the light from the projector to appear. When the picture finally came on, I couldn't believe my eyes.

Before most of us realized what was happening, several Marines had charged the projectionist, snatched the projector and threw it on the ground. It was a free for all. Several days of pent-up tensions had suddenly boiled over. It took the officers and staff NCO's a good twenty minutes to break up the fight. More Marines were injured during that outbreak than during the preceding two days of enemy shelling. The whole incident probably would have never taken place if some jerk in the rear hadn't thought that a bunch of combat weary Marines might enjoy seeing John Wayne starring in The Green Berets. The free for all wasn't treated as a racial incident, although that's what it was in reality. Once the fighting began, it turned into a black vs. white conflict.

The next morning, things seemed to be back to normal. Well, as normal as things ever were in Vietnam. We sent out our patrols, set up our ambushes and hoped that Charlie felt like fighting today. Our battalion commander knew the only way he could defuse racial tensions was to send as many Marines on patrol as possible. We were in-between operations and the worst thing you could have in Vietnam was a bunch of angry combat veterans sitting around with nothing to do. None of the patrols made contact with the enemy all day.

When we returned to Vandergrift, we were met with a strange order. Everyone below the rank of sergeant was to turn in his ammunition at the gates of the base. We were assured that in case of an attack, our ammunition would be reissued in plenty of time. I couldn't believe it. There we were in the middle of nowhere, surrounded by North Vietnamese regulars and Viet Cong and they were taking our ammunition.

This war grows stranger by the minute, I thought, as I dumped my loaded magazines into one of the barrels placed just inside the gate for that purpose.

I headed for my tent, dropped my gear and stretched out on my cot. My thoughts drifted back to the Vietnamese villager who had thrown the grenade into Johnson's chopper eight days earlier. He had worked at the base for months and no one had suspected that he was a Viet Cong, more than willing to sacrifice his life for his cause. How many others who worked on the base are also Viet Cong, I wondered as I closed my eyes.

After the chopper carrying Johnson was blown up, an added security measure went into effect. All male villagers were restricted from the base. Only females and children were allowed to enter, and they had to be off base by sunset. I laughed to myself when I thought about how a Vietnamese woman, or a child could kill you just as easily as a man. These were people who had been fighting all their lives. Death was no stranger to them. To give their life for their cause was an honor. Nevertheless, it was felt that we were safer if the local male population was restricted from the base. I had only been back at the tent a few minutes when Lieutenant Smith walked in. One of the newly arrived replacements shouted. "Attention!"

The rest of us just looked at him like he was crazy. Several of us laughed at the nervous new guy standing at attention, waiting for Lieutenant Smith to return his salute.

"At ease, private. Around here we don't stand on formality. If you ever salute me in the bush, I'll personally break your arm," Lieutenant Smith said as he returned the salute. In the bush, an officer didn't exactly want to go around advertising his rank.

"How come they made us turn in our ammo sir?" Bass inquired.

"The Colonel is afraid that after yesterday, you guys might open fire on each other. So as a precaution, he gave the order to collect all ammo."

The Lieutenant's answer was met with a series of grumbles and whispers. It was just another example of the insanity that went on in Vietnam.

"I do have some good news, however. The whole platoon has been given a forty-eight hour pass to Da Nang." The words had barely escaped Lieutenant Smith's mouth when everyone began shouting and cheering. "Hold it down. Hold it down," he shouted in an attempt to restore order.

It took a full two minutes before everyone was calm enough for Lieutenant Smith to continue. "I hate to disappoint those of you who arrived in the past few days." His last remark was addressed to the five replacements, waiting in the tent when we returned from our patrol. "You'll have to stay behind and keep an eye on things while the rest of the platoon goes on leave. If you're going to take advantage of the skipper's kindness, the trucks will be loading at zero six hundred. Anyone not ready to leave on time will get left behind. Those of you authorized to carry side arms may wear them. You'll be issued ammo as you board the trucks, but the chamber is to remain clear. Is that understood?"

Since I was now a squad leader, in addition to my M-16, I carried a forty-five. Although I knew that you didn't need to walk around Da Nang armed, I felt better knowing that I would have a weapon with me. "Yes sir," I answered, along with the three other squad leaders.

"I am holding each squad leader personally responsible for the conduct of each member of his squad while in Da Nang. Keep an eye out for con artists, pick pockets, and the clap. Enjoy yourselves and I'll see you Thursday."

No sooner had the lieutenant stepped out of the tent, than everyone began shouting and yelling again.

"Are you ready for Da Nang?" I asked Bass.

"I'm not going with you," was his surprising answer.

"What do you mean, you're not going?" I asked, somewhat puzzled.

148

"Just what I said. Read my lips," he said slowly, as he emphasized his earlier words. "I'm not going!"

"Why not?"

"Because, you might have momentarily forgotten that as of next Saturday, this war is history for me. I'm not going anywhere except to the mess tent and the showers between now and then. You enjoy yourself because there is no telling when you'll get the chance again."

"I'd probably do the same thing if was me going back to the real-world next Saturday," I said enthusiastically in an attempt to conceal my disappointment. "It would have been nice to party together before you left."

Bass smiled, then reached into his pocket and pulled out a large wad of military payment certificates. Military payment certificates were what we were paid with instead of good old U.S. green dollars. It was a form of currency control. Although less desirable than U.S. dollars in Da Nang, they spent almost as well.

"Have a good time for me and for Johnson, little brother," Bass said to me, as he handed me the certificates.

"I can't take these. There must be several thousand dollars here," I blurted out.

"Forty-five hundred, to be exact. I don't feel like explaining to anyone where I got them, if I tried to exchange them. Buy all the fellows at least one drink, and then piss off the rest. Have the time of your life, and spend every dime of it for me and Johnson."

"I sure will. Thanks a lot," I said gratefully.

Bass stretched out on his cot, placed his hands behind his head and closed his eyes. "Thank me by painting the town red. Knock yourself out."

I said no more. By now, I knew Bass quite well. He had a way of letting you know when he was finished talking and when he wanted to be left alone. I got his message. I tucked the certificates deep inside my sea bag, making sure no one saw me, then headed for the showers.

In less than twenty minutes, I was back in the tent stretched out on my cot again. I thought of the many stories Johnson and Bass had told me about the good times they had in Da Nang, and had been looking forward to my first leisure trip there. But the fact Bass wasn't going with me, and the still fresh memories of Johnson's tragic death put a slight damper on the anticipated trip. Still, I looked forward to seeing the infamous Da Nang night life. Before I drifted to sleep, I vowed to turn Da Nang out for Johnson and Bass.

CHAPTER TWELVE

The first thing I did when I arrived in Da Nang was fulfill Bass's request. I bought the entire platoon several rounds at a local bar. We saluted Johnson, Bass and all the other brave men who had served with the Walking Dead. Next, we saluted ourselves and the poor unfortunate bastards who would follow.

Da Nang was everything I imagined it to be and much more. It was like a living, breathing kaleidoscope. From corner to corner, things changed completely. The city was abundant in wealth, poverty, sin, and sights that reminded me of the war going on. The main drag reminded me of the description given of 42nd Street in New York City, by the men in the unit who had never been there. I amused myself with the thought that the neon sign maker must be the wealthiest man in all Da Nang.

Neon signs were everywhere. I thought New York City lit up at night, but this place took the cake. Names like Club Prince, Show club Harbor Lights, Club King and countless others seemed to jump out at me. It was barely ten a.m., and already the streets were filled with thousands of Vietnamese moving about alongside thousands of U.S. military personnel out for a good time.

Although I was well liked by everyone in the platoon, I hadn't become too friendly with anyone except Johnson and Bass. After paying for the drinks, I politely turned down several offers to hang out with one group of fellows or another. I wanted to hang with myself. Besides, the only thing on the minds of a good ninety percent of the guys was getting laid. There was plenty of opportunity for that in Da Nang. If they had been putting "softpeter" in our food, it sure wore off quickly. I exited the bar, and hadn't gone the equivalent of two city blocks before I was propositioned twice.

"Hey, GI, you want I show you a good time?" "Hi ya, handsome, you want to get laid?"

Each time I was approached, I simply shook my head no and kept on my way. Now don't get me wrong, I was as horny as the next guy was. Call me overly cautious. Call me gullible. Call me what you like. I wasn't going to chance catching any of the dreaded social diseases I heard so much about. Numerous stories about the strange varieties of venereal diseases that one could easily catch in Vietnam circulated everywhere. If that wasn't enough of a deterrent, I reminded myself of the many stories about how the women stuck all sorts of things up their vaginas to harm you. Nope, not me, I wasn't chancing it. Of course, I didn't tell that to any of the other guys. I simply gave them a story about having to catch up with an old friend from back home, then set out on my own to explore this fascinating city.

The thing that struck me first was the American influence that was everywhere. I'm not just talking about the obvious military presence. You could see America in the clothing worn by the people of Da Nang, you could see it in the store windows, and you could even see it in the actions of the people. I had thought that Macys's department store back in New York was well stocked and offered a wide range of choices, but compared to the shops in Da Nang, Macys's product line was extremely limited. The shops were overflowing with electronic goods and other items that American servicemen couldn't seem to get enough of. Their prices couldn't be beat either. If you were paying in U.S. dollars instead of military payment certificates, you could almost triple your buying power.

In Da Nang, the expression "money talks" took on a whole new meaning. You could see a spillover of the entire social fiber of America in Da Nang. The people were good at imitating the American way of life, right on down to the segregation that existed in America.

At first, I was surprised to discover that in Da Nang, as in just about every large city in America, there was the neighborhood that catered to whites and a separate one for blacks. It really freaked me out. In the neighborhood that catered to white servicemen, the Vietnamese there imitated white Americans quite well. They talked like them, walked like them, played their kind of music and danced like them. Beatles and Stones music could be heard blasting from the clubs and the bars.

In the neighborhood that catered to black servicemen you were greeted with extended palms and choruses of "What's happening, brother!" Songs by the Temptations, Jackson Five and James Brown blared from the numerous bars and electronic shops. There was one song that occasionally played well on both sides of town. In-A-Gadda-Da-Vida by Iron Butterfly was the only cross-over song. It was sort of the unofficial anthem of the men in Vietnam. As I continued my stroll, I couldn't help but think about how deep American influence ran. Here we were in Vietnam, fighting to help them preserve their freedom and civil rights. The irony of it all was that everywhere I looked I saw reminders of the struggle back home for freedom and civil rights. I shook my head. The Vietnamese had adopted American ways quite well, I concluded.

It was still early in the day. I made a mental list of the many things I wanted to do. First, I wanted to check out some real Vietnamese cooking, then just walk around and get a good look at Da Nang and its many contrasting lifestyles. Most importantly, I wanted to visit a special place Johnson had told me about.

I ventured upon a Vietnamese restaurant with highly appetizing aromas filtering from the entrance and decided to try it out. More than an hour had passed by the time I wiped the last few crumbs from my mouth. The meal I had just devoured was, without a doubt, one of the finest I'd ever eaten. The cuisine was everything I had been told to expect. I stuffed myself until I felt my stomach would burst. Thanks to Bass, I was loaded and could easily afford any and every luxury the city had to offer. I complemented my meal with a bottle of the finest wine available. For two hundred dollars in M.P.C.'s, I enjoyed the best French wine to be found in Da Nang. Before leaving the restaurant, I ordered another bottle of the same, to go.

The next several hours, I just free floated around the city. I was awed by the many different sights and sounds of life in hypnotic Da Nang. I lost track of the number of times I was propositioned, offered drugs to buy, or asked if I wanted a good deal on exchanging my money. It didn't take me long to realize that the largest market in Da Nang was the black market. If you wanted something available anywhere on earth, you could get it with the right connection. By three in the afternoon, I had seen enough of the city.

Aside from the meal, my only other purchase was a double lens reflex, thirty-five millimeter camera and two rolls of film. The shop owner threw in a camera case as a gift. While I was putting my newly purchased camera into the case, I couldn't help but chuckle as I thought, here I am in Da Nang, South Vietnam buying a camera made in Japan, which fits snugly in a case made in Hong Kong. So, to keep up the international spirit of things, I declined a free roll of some brand X film and instead purchased a couple of rolls of good old Kodak. The shop owner spoke a fair amount of English, so I handed him a piece of paper with an address scribbled on it and inquired if he knew how to get there. He did and, with a little difficulty, he was able to direct me. It was not too far outside the other side of town.

After thanking the electronics shop owner for his directions and advice I made a hasty exit. I had one more purchase to make. I darted into a grocery store next to the electronic shop, purchased several loaves of bread, some cheese and a large variety of candies. I paid for my purchase and thanked the shop owner, then exited the shop and hailed a cab. Actually, I didn't have to hail one. They were everywhere. I was barely seated in the cab when the driver began to bombard me with a series of statement-like questions. "You want nice girl? You want to buy some grass? You want trade American dollars?"

I listened to him babble on for a good minute or so before cutting him off. "No thanks. I just want to get to this address," I stated flatly as I handed him the piece of paper. "Do you know how to get there?

"No sweat. You sure you no want nice girl?"

"I'm sure. Just take me to that address," I repeated.

The shop owner had been pretty thorough in describing how to get there and had expressed some concern that a cab driver might take me for an unnecessarily long ride. As a precaution, he described a number of signs I should look out for. It was obvious the cab driver made more money hustling than he did from driving his cab. After twenty minutes of slow moving in and out of a maze of military vehicles, jeeps, cars, scooters, bikes, rickshaws and pedestrians, the cab driver pulled up in front of a long stone fence.

"Is this it?" I asked.

The driver nodded his head. I didn't bother asking him how much the fare was. Instead, I handed him twenty dollars in MPCs. He was obviously both surprised and grateful. He nodded his head up and down, repeating, "Thank you. Thank you."

I carefully looked to the left and to the right before entering an archway into an enclosed yard. The gray stone fence ran at least fifty yards in each direction around the yard. I entered, then stopped just on the other side of the archway. About twenty yards, directly in front of me, stood a large house.

It was a two-story house, made of stone similar to that used to make the fence. It was adorned with a dingy white roof and faded white shutters on the windows. I continued on and heard the sounds of laughing children coming from somewhere in back of the house. A man appeared in the doorway, just as I reached the house. At first, I thought that he was an American. He appeared to be in his late fifties or early sixties. His head was full of gray hair, which glistened in the afternoon sunlight. When he spoke, I recognized his French accent. "Good afternoon. May I help you?"

"Hi, my name is Richard Henry. I'm a friend of Corporal Freddie Johnson."

At the mention of Johnson's name, the Frenchman cut me off. "Ah, Corporal Johnson. Do come in. How is my good friend?" he asked, as he motioned me into the house.

The look on my face in response to his question must have given away my thoughts at the moment. Before I could say anything, he addressed me again.

"He is not so okay?" he asked in a tone that indicated that he suspected the worse.

"He's dead," I replied.

The distinguished looking Frenchman made no attempt to hide his hurt and sadness. Several tears rolled down his cheeks. "Johnson, he was a good man. He was a good friend to me and to the children. How did he die?"

I proceeded to recount the tragic scene and while telling the story, had a troubling thought. Why did people always want to know the intimate details of how someone died? Did it really matter how someone got killed in Vietnam?

Very often, after the families of those killed in combat received news of the death of their dearly, or sometimes not so dearly beloved via an early morning knock on their door, they would write a friend of the deceased to ask for details of the circumstances surrounding their death.

After a good hour of conversation, I knew all about the Frenchman and how he came to know and consider Johnson such a dear friend. Chevalier was born and raised in Vietnam. His father was a former French official. Prior to World War II, he had worked for the French government. After the war, he went into the import and export business. He made a lot of money and shared his wealth with the local villagers, providing food for the hungry and purchasing medicine for the local hospital. Because of his generosity, he had managed to survive the ill fate that befell many French Nationals who lived in Vietnam during the years of fighting with the French. He considered himself Vietnamese and so did the people in and around Da Nang who knew him.

His wife had passed away several years earlier and he had devoted the past three years of his life to taking care of children who were products of a Vietnamese mother and an American father. Internationally, they were called Amerasians. If the father was black, in Vietnam, they were called "bui doi," meaning "children of the dust."

Although his home was a haven for any child in need of shelter, fifteen of the infants and toddlers that he cared for were fathered by black American servicemen. In addition to the infants and toddlers, several older children, ranging in ages from six to sixteen, lived in Chevalier's unofficial children's home.

Johnson had met Chevalier almost a year earlier while on his first R&R in Da Nang. The first night of his leave, while walking down the street, he had spied a young Vietnamese woman carrying a baby tightly in her arms. She looked scared, lost and alone. Johnson approached her and struck up a conversation. To his surprise, she spoke a fairly decent amount of English and they had little trouble understanding one another. The young woman explained how her friend had just given birth a few days ago to the baby she was carrying. The baby's mother, her friend, had died earlier in the day from complications related to the child's birth. They hadn't sought medical help because her friend hadn't wanted anyone to know she had given birth to a half black child. To be a prostitute was okay, but to give birth to a black child was unforgivable.

The young woman Johnson just befriended explained to him that she had heard about a Frenchman who lived in a big house on the other side of town and cared for such children. She went on to tell Johnson that she was on her way to take the baby boy to him. She was scared that someone might see her, and she lacked money to take a cab. Johnson offered to accompany her, and she gladly accepted. Chevalier went on to tell me how moved Johnson was by what he saw at his house.

Several weeks after Johnson returned to One-Nine, Chevalier received a letter from him containing several hundred dollars. After that, once a month, he would receive a letter from Johnson containing money.

The letters were always the same. All Johnson wrote was Dear Frenchie, I hope you and the little ones are hanging in there. He always signed it Peace, FJ. He visited Chevalier several times during the following ten months. "Whenever he arrived, it was like Christmas for the little ones. He brought lots of toys and other treats for them." When he was done telling me about how he had come to know and befriend Johnson, he paused for a moment. Tears began to flow freely down his cheeks for a few seconds before he wiped his face dry on his shoulders. Before I had the opportunity to respond to what he had told me, he stood up and addressed me. "Come, you must see and meet the children."

I reached into the shopping bag I had brought with me and pulled out the bread and wine. "Perhaps later, we can break bread together and drink a glass of wine?"

"I would like that very much. But first, you must meet my family."

I grabbed the bag containing the candy and followed Chevalier through the house out into a courtyard. Several toddlers were playing under the watchful eyes of a couple of older children. Protected by the shade of two large trees there were several cribs, each with a couple of infants in them. Two Vietnamese women, who appeared to be in their early twenties, were tending to them.

"This is my family," he said proudly, as he pointed to the children.

Immediately upon seeing him, two of the toddlers ran over and clung to his trouser legs. Chevalier reached down and picked them up, one in each arm. Neither appeared to be quite four years old.

"Tom, Bobby, say hello to our friend, Mr. Henry." I looked at the two little boys.

"Hi," I said, smiling. I was a stranger to them, and I didn't expect them to return my greeting or to warm up to me immediately and, thus, was quite surprised when one tot returned my smile and extended his arms toward me. I reached out and took him in my arms. Right then and there, he won my heart for himself and all the other children at Chevalier's home. He had the brightest brown eyes I'd ever seen. His skin was creamy, and his smile was enough to melt the most hardened of hearts.

"When they are brought here, or when I find one of them abandoned in an alley somewhere, they are usually too young to speak and tell me their names, if they even have one. There is no hiding what they are, so I give them American first names. All the children that are half American are looked down on. The ones whose fathers are white are a little luckier than the ones with black fathers. The ones with black fathers are considered to be less than dirt and no one will have anything to do with them. Look at these children. Are they responsible for what they are? Have you ever seen more beautiful children?"

I gazed around at the faces of several children who, by now, had gathered around me. I could see their disappointment when they realized that I wasn't their friend Corporal Johnson. Still, their eyes sparkled.

"You're absolutely right, Chevalier, they're all beautiful."

I knelt down, still holding Tom, who was clinging tightly to my neck. Several children walked over to me and began smiling.

"Say hello to our friend, children," Chevalier instructed them.

Those who understood him either said "Hi" or shyly waved their tiny fingers in a gesture that stood for hello.

After setting Tom down, one by one, I handed each of them a piece of candy.

"Say thank you, children. Remember your manners."

Again, those who understood and could talk, obeyed Chevalier, and thanked me. I didn't need to hear any of them

161

say thanks. Their sweet, angelic, innocent, smiling faces thanked me in more ways than I could count.

"Run and play now, children."

Obediently, several of them began to skip across the yard. All the other children soon followed, except two; Tom, who had released his hold on me long enough to unwrap his candy and another little girl who appeared to be around the same age. Neither budged an inch. They just stood there, looking directly at me with four bright clear eyes.

"I said run along, children."

"It's okay," I quickly interjected. I sat on the ground, then motioned for the two to come sit on my lap. Tom didn't hesitate to jump onto it. The little girl just stood there, staring, smiling broadly at me.

"What's your name?" I asked.

In response to my question, she only smiled more.

"Her name is Miriko. It does my heart good to see her smile. This is the first time that I have seen her really smile since I brought her here. I found her wandering the streets early one morning a year ago. She hasn't said a word since she has been here. There is a doctor who works at the hospital who comes around once a month. He took her to the hospital for some tests a few months back and couldn't find anything physically wrong with her. Actually, she is quite bright. I watch her a lot. She is a quick learner."

While Chevalier was speaking to me, Miriko walked over and climbed onto my lap next to Tom.

"Hi Miriko. My name is Richard."

I didn't expect an answer, but I was surprised and delighted when she leaned over and kissed me on my cheek.

"It looks like you're just what the doctor ordered. I have never seen her warmup to anyone before."

"Miriko, that's not a Vietnamese or an American name. How did she get it?"

"Actually, it is American. I named her after a Japanese-American nurse who used to spend her free time here with the children. She was a Naval lieutenant and returned to the states a couple of months ago. Like Johnson, she was a rare individual. Judging by the way those two have taken to you, I suspect that you are, also."

"Thanks, but it is the children who are rare and precious. After all, isn't this whole damn stinking war about their future?" I blurted out without giving much thought to my angry delivery. "I apologize for my tone just then," I added quickly.

"There is no need. These children have no real future, unless I can figure out a way to get them to America. Their compatriots will never accept them. Enough about that. Come meet the rest of my family."

Chevalier walked me around the courtyard and introduced me to several older children and a couple of Vietnamese women. He explained how they were a tremendous help with the infants and toddlers. The two women were from a small hamlet not too far from Da Nang and came daily to help. All the while we walked and talked, Tom and Miriko rested snugly in my arms. Tom pointed at various things around the yard and proudly called them by name, while Miriko just kept smiling and playing with my collar insignias.

163

After a good ten minutes, Chevalier suggested that we return to the house, uncork the bottle of wine and toast Johnson. I bent slightly and returned Tom and Miriko to the ground. When his feet touched the ground, Tom wasted no time in skipping off to join the other children. Miriko however, wrapped her hands tightly around my neck and held on for dear life. Then her smile turned to a look of sadness and fear. I held onto her, stood up and gave her a hug. "It's okay, Miriko. I'm not going anywhere. I'll be right inside."

I didn't know if she understood, or if it made any difference. I just didn't know what else to say or do. I looked at Chevalier, a blank expression on my face. He returned my look with a soft smile, then called out to an older child, who immediately ran over to where we stood.

"Take Miriko over with the other children."

The teenager reached out, gripped Miriko's waist and wound up having to pry her tiny arms from around my neck. All the time she was crying and fighting to hang on. I felt helpless because I wanted to keep her with me, but figured Chevalier knew best.

Ten minutes later, Chevalier and I were seated in the house, toasting Johnson. I made an offer to run back into Da Nang and get everything necessary for a large dinner and party for everyone. Chevalier accepted my offer only after I agreed to spend the night.

One of the women from the hamlet went with me to Da Nang and with her help, I made sure each of the children had a new change of clothing complete with shoes. In addition, I bought a toy for each and a supply of brightly colored wrapping paper, ribbon and bows. We returned to the house in a taxi.

While Chevalier and one of the women prepared supper, the woman who had gone shopping with me helped wrap the gifts for the children. She took care in seeing to it that each had the correct name tag attached. I had made a special purchase for Miriko. It was a little music box shaped like an old-fashioned phonograph. When you wound up the crank, it played Greensleeves. I listened to the tune once before I tucked the music box neatly into a gift box, then wrapped and decorated it.

It was seven-thirty when we finally sat down to supper. It was indeed a grand meal. The food far surpassed the meal I'd eaten earlier at the restaurant in town. In fact, there was no comparison. There was plenty for everyone. For dessert we had chocolate cake. I insisted that Chevalier let the children eat as much as they wanted.

After supper, Chevalier instructed the older ones to take the younger children into the courtyard and seat them in a circle. A few minutes later, we joined them. Their bright eyes seemed to light up as they spied the bags full of presents, we carried. The two women from the nearby hamlet joined us and, one by one, we gave the children their presents. I couldn't begin to describe the joy and excitement that could be seen and felt when the children opened their gifts.

We made a game out of it. After I handed out the first present, everyone waited until it was opened, then they all clapped. The child who had just opened a gift would thank me, then reach into the pile of presents and hand me the next one. I would call off the name on the gift and the procedure was repeated until all the presents had been handed out, except my special gift for Miriko.

Just as I expected she would, when all the other children were excused and went off to try on their new clothing or play with their new toys, Miriko walked over to me and stood there smiling broadly. She was clutching tightly to the doll she had received moments earlier. I lifted her and sat her on my lap. She kissed me on my cheek as she had done earlier. I reached into my pocket and pulled out the special gift I had for her.

"What's this?" I asked playfully.

Miriko hesitated a moment before taking the present. Chevalier and I looked at each other, then back at her while she struggled to open her gift. She tried in vain, before handing it back to me. I pulled off the bow, and stuck it to her hair. She patted it atop her head and widened her smile. I opened the gift and showed Miriko how to wind up the music box. When I handed it back to her, she placed it next to her ear and listened.

When the music box wound down, she rewound it and held it close to my ear. Once the music box was silenced again, Miriko clutched it tightly and rested her head on my shoulder. Chevalier and I continued to chat awhile. I hadn't noticed that Miriko had fallen asleep, until Chevalier called it to my attention. "Ah, look at the pretty angel. She is fast asleep. I will summon one of the children to carry her to bed."

"Is it all right if I put her to bed and tuck her in?" "Sure, follow me. I'll show you to her room."

The room was decorated with reminders of childhood. On one wall were pictures of animals. On another hung a brightly colored rainbow. A third was decorated with a painting of a South Vietnamese and an American flag. Although I understood the significance, I couldn't help but become angry at seeing the two together in one painting. Gently I placed Miriko in her bed and pulled a sheet over her. She was a product of our two nations coming together. More likely than not, she would have to pay for that the rest of her life. I stood looking at her while Chevalier checked on the other sleeping children in the room. When he returned to where I stood, I bent down and gently kissed Miriko on her forehead.

"Come, my friend. Let us go relax and share a bottle of wine. You have done much for the children today. For Miriko, you have done much more than I can ever thank you for."

"You don't have to thank me. Seeing her and all the other children smile is thanks enough."

Chevalier and I sat around sipping wine and munching on bite-sized chunks of cheese until the wee hours of the morning. I was fascinated by the stories he told me about the Vietnamese people and Vietnam. He was sure that the war would end only when the two Vietnams were one again.

"It has nothing to do with politics. Most of the people are not concerned with the politics of this war. They are a strong-willed people and, for centuries, have never accepted foreign dominance. They never will. You cannot fight the will of a people. Now don't get me wrong. I sincerely believe that America believes She is right in being over here. I also believe that America has come to believe what She has, based on misinformation."

The manner in which he referred to America struck me as strange. I had never before heard anyone speak of it in such all-encompassing terms. The America I had grown up in was a country in which there was a clear division of black and white. When I finally lay down to rest, it took what seemed like forever to fall asleep. I lay in bed wondering what the future held for Chevalier's family. I finally fell asleep thinking about what I could do after I got home to call attention to the plight of children such as the ones, I had met that day.

The remainder of my leave was spent as a guest at Chevalier's home. I spent most of next day playing with the children. Throughout the day, Miriko stuck by me like glue. The only time she wasn't close by my side was when Chevalier and I went into town the second evening that I was there. First, he took me on a grand tour of Da Nang, and then we had supper with two of his friends.

The couple was also French. Both appeared to be around the same age as Chevalier. Just like him, they had been born in Vietnam and it was the only home they had ever known. Unlike Chevalier, they had begun making preparations to leave the country soon. They were convinced the war was lost and equally convinced that the North Vietnamese would not be as kind to them as their South Vietnamese compatriots had been. Like Chevalier, they too had seen the French ousted by the Japanese, who themselves were replaced by the French again after World War II.

To this day, I remember a statement the elderly gentleman made. It was a short one that would stick with me the remainder of my tour in Vietnam.

"You cannot win a war that was lost before it began. You can only hope to survive it."

It was rather late when we returned to the house. All the infants and younger children had gone to sleep. All except Miriko. She was sitting on the floor near the entrance to the dining room, playing with her music box. She looked so cute sitting there, dressed in the outfit I had given her the previous day. We were greeted by one of the teenagers. "I could not get her to stay in her bed. Twice, I undressed her and put her to bed and twice, she dressed herself again and climbed back out."

Immediately upon seeing me, Miriko ran over and extended her arms, motioning for me to pick her up. I think I was as happy to see her smiling face as she was to see mine, even if I had never seen her before yesterday. In my heart, I knew I was someone special to her and she to me. I looked into her soft bright eyes and fought back tears.

My forty-eight hours of R&R would soon be over. I would be leaving early in the morning, long before Miriko or any of the other children would be awake. I wished with all my might that, at that very moment, the war would end, and I could head home, taking this innocent child of God with me.

In war, there are many kinds of pain. It hurt knowing that in a few short hours, I would have to leave Miriko, Tom and the other children whom I had come to know and love in so short a time.

Chevalier accompanied me to Miriko's bedside. I helped her undress and when she was ready for bed, I gave her a big hug. She hugged me back. I laid her in bed and pulled her sheet up over her shoulders. When I bent over to kiss her good night, both Chevalier and I were stunned as she sat up, threw her arms around me and in a low but clear voice said,

"Good night."

Mariko released her hold on my neck, returned her head to her pillow and closed her eyes. I was taken by surprise, but Chevalier looked flabbergasted. This time, I couldn't hold back my tears. I whispered good night to her, quickly turned away and exited the room. Chevalier followed me out. His voice cracked when he spoke again.

"It is the first time I have ever heard her speak. Some of the children have told me they have heard her talk before, but I have never heard her utter a word, until now!"

I looked over at him in time to see him wipe a tear from his cheek. I was no longer upset that I had been unable to stop my tears.

"God, it's going to be hard leaving here in the morning. I'll miss all the children, especially Mariko."

"You must return to your unit. We will be with you in spirit. We will pray that you stay well and that you will come see us again."

"I'll be back as soon and as often as I can. Would you do me a favor?"

"Sure, if I can."

"If I leave my camera here until I come back, will you take a few pictures of everyone and send them to me?"

"Of course. But first, let me take a few pictures of you. I think that they will be good for Miriko to have."

After snapping several pictures of me, Chevalier selected a bottle of wine from his collection of excellent French wines.

He proposed a toast to my wellbeing and I proposed one to his and the children's. We were almost through consuming the bottle of wine, when I reached in my pocket and pulled out what was left of the military payment certificates Bass had given me, along with several hundred dollars of my own.

"I almost forgot. Johnson asked me to give you this. He gave it to me the day before he got killed. He said to tell you he was sorry he couldn't get by to see you and the children before he left."

I sensed that Chevalier knew I was fabricating that story. He stared at me a long time before taking the money from my extended hand.

"You are indeed a very special person, Monsieur Henry. I thank you for the children and for myself."

"Thank Johnson," I replied.

Chevalier winked, nodded his head and raised his glass high above his head. "To Corporal Johnson, may he rest in peace. And to you. May your kindness be returned throughout your life."

"And may it be a long life," I added. I cracked a smile and tapped my glass on his.

"And may it be a long life," Chevalier repeated.

He returned my smile. Simultaneously we took a sip, then gulped down the remainder of wine.

"Well, my friend. I best be getting to bed. I have to catch a truck at seven."

"Sleep well, Monsieur Henry. I will see to it that you are awakened in plenty of time."

"Thanks. Good night."

I extended my hand and tightly gripped his. We shook hands firmly.

"Do not worry about Miriko. Her life is already better for your having entered it."

In silence, I placed my empty glass on the table in front of me and retreated to my room.

CHAPTER THIRTEEN

When I returned to Vandergrift, much to my relief, there was no time to sit around and think about the past few days I had spent in Da Nang. The regiment had just received word that it was assigned to spearhead a new campaign code named Utah Mesa. It didn't surprise me when I learned the One-Nine would be the first to move out. We arrived back at the base close to ten hundred hours and had to be ready to pull out by fourteen hundred hours. The entire 9th Regimental Landing Team, with support units from the 26th Marines, would be involved in operation Utah Mesa. We were told that the basic thrust of the operation was to run a sweep for Viet Cong through a twenty- square-kilometer area. We were to search every village and hamlet in the designated area.

I was a little disappointed upon learning that Bass had left for home the day before I returned from R&R. Because he was a real short-timer, he wasn't going to participate in the upcoming operation. Headquarters cut his orders for the real world a few days early. I would have liked to say goodbye face to face. Still, I was glad that he finally got to go home. By thirteen forty, my entire battalion was gathered in the designated staging area, ready to begin Operation Utah Mesa. We would be climbing aboard the waiting choppers in a few minutes. Once in the bush, we would split up into platoon-sized units. Each platoon would be charged with searching and clearing a given area. By dusk, the platoons would rendezvous at a set of predetermined coordinates, where the battalion would set up camp for the night.

It seemed simple enough, but as usual, there was a catch. We were reminded that some of the villages and hamlets were designated "No Fire Zones." That meant they were supposed to be friendly, as in loyal to the government of The Republic of South Vietnam. Even if we were fired upon when entering a "friendly" village or hamlet, we were to refrain from returning fire. Instead, we were to assume that any rounds that were shot at us came from one or two snipers, and we were expected to search them out without endangering the civilian population. After all, part of the new strategy in Vietnam was "to win the heart and minds of the people."

The whole idea of a "No Fire Zone" struck me as ludicrous. If the villagers were so damn loyal to the government of the Republic of South Vietnam, why the hell were they harboring Viet Cong? Who were the Viet Cong anyway? They were, of course, the people of the so-called friendly villages. They gave the appearance of being friendly by day, but were in reality, extremely deadly by night. We were also told that a few of the villages and hamlets were known Viet Cong sanctuaries. These villages were to be searched and destroyed. When the term "Search and Destroy" was used, it generally meant that no one from the rear would be monitoring our activities in the bush. So, if we received hostile fire, we were free to deal with it in any way we chose. That usually meant shooting anything that moved, then setting the place on fire with a flick of our trusty Zippo lighters.

174

Most of the real short timers, those with less than two weeks left in country, were transferred to the rear, then were replaced by a bunch of Marines fresh from the states. As a result, nearly half the men in my battalion would be going to the bush for the first time. If that wasn't bad enough, the number of replacements assigned to my platoon was higher than the battalion average. Close to seventy percent of the men in the second platoon lacked combat experience. So I found myself in charge of a squad full of untried Marines. Besides myself, there were only two other Marines assigned to my squad who had any combat experience.

I briefed my squad in an attempt to calm their nerves. "Relax and do as you're told. Keep alert and with a little luck, we'll be back here before you know it. Don't cluster up out there and be on the lookout for signs of mines or booby traps. They'll kill you quicker than Charlie."

By the looks on the faces of my squad members, I realized that my little pep talk was adding to their nervousness.

"We've been through the area a few times before, so in all likelihood, we won't run up on much."

Although I told that to my squad members, I knew better. In fact, as far as I knew, the area we were about to drop into hadn't been swept in at least six months and was really hot.

Judging by the size of the operation we were about to embark on, I could tell that it wasn't going to be a picnic. Despite what the Captain had told us, I knew we weren't simply going to check out a few villages and hamlets. We weren't searching for a handful of VC, either. We were going to bump heads with a well-entrenched force of NVA somewhere. There didn't seem to be any point in worrying a

175

bunch of rookies. Besides, I knew that once the shit hit the fan, my new charges would come through just as I had my first time out. The waiting game was what wore you down the most in the bush. Although I couldn't see them, I could sense the enemy presence while we conducted our patrols the first two days of Utah Mesa. They were out there, all around us and nowhere at the same time.

Still, our platoon hadn't made contact with any enemy forces. The first and third platoons had a brief encounter with separate small units of North Vietnamese regulars during the second day of the operation. Four Marines were injured. Fortunately, all of them had minor cuts from shrapnel. They did manage to kill three enemy soldiers. After we joined up that evening, I listened to descriptions of the gear the North Vietnamese soldiers were carrying. It was clear they were expecting us.

When we did make full contact with them, it was a good bet we would have to drive them from strongly defended, well concealed and heavily fortified positions. The fact that we ran up on a couple of their units conducting patrols of their own told us something. The swiftness with which we mounted Operation Utah Mesa caught the enemy off-guard. Although we couldn't conceal our arrival in the area, the NVA lacked any way of telling how many of us there were or how heavily armed we were. That could be an advantage or disadvantage. It all depended on how the enemy interpreted their reconnaissance reports. Since we were operating during the day in platoon sized units, it would be difficult for the North Vietnamese to get correct numbers on us. To insure that they couldn't get close enough to see how large our forces were, we set up several ambushes around our camp and a good number of sentries were on duty at all times.

On the second night of Operation Utah Mesa, the mortar and rocket attacks began and continued at regular intervals throughout the night. Most of the rockets fell short of their intended mark and the vast majority of the artillery shells slammed into the jungle to our rear. Thus far, we had been successful in keeping the enemy reconnaissance patrols from pinpointing our exact location.

Soon the enemy would have to come out into the open in order to engage us in battle. If they remained hidden much longer, one of our patrols would stumble across their base of operations. Although our unit might get caught by surprise, there was no way they could cut down a heavily armed company of Marines before reinforcements and air support could be called in. The way Captain Jenkins figured it the NVA would wait us out for another day or two, then come at us full force on the morning of the third or fourth day of the operation. They would shell us just before sunrise, then try and overrun our bivouac area.

The next morning, Lieutenant Colonel Gibbs, the new battalion commander, decided we would patrol in squad sized units. We would run most of our patrols near our base camp. This way we could insure that the enemy kept far away from us until they were ready to launch their anticipated full attack. In order to keep Charlie occupied and unsuspecting, at least one platoon would be sent out on a long-range patrol. Search and clear operation my ass! My original suspicions were correct. The primary objective of our operation was to draw the enemy out into the open.

My platoon was given the assignment of going on one of the long range "nuisance" patrols, and as Lieutenant Smith put it, "Making ourselves heard." That meant we were expected to hike through the jungle all day, just to keep the North Vietnamese patrols on their toes and away from our base camp. Colonel Gibbs was preparing his own surprise for the enemy when they launched their attack. He was absolutely sure the attack would begin in two days at dawn.

It was miserable. It hadn't rained in several days and by ten a.m. the heat was almost unbearable. After patrolling for several hours, most of the men in the platoon were drenched in sweat. I took quite a few salt tablets, but they didn't seem to help. We would be out in the sun and heat all day, so we had to conserve our drinking water.

At ten thirty, the Lieutenant decided we needed a rest. He was a veteran of many operations and knew when to push us and when to rest us. After selecting a relatively safe area, the Lieutenant summoned the squad leaders for a briefing. Since it was left to his discretion how he ran the patrol, he thought it best that instead of the entire platoon patrolling in one direction, we would continue as two units. He would take charge of the third and fourth squads and SSgt. Brisslow would take command of the first and second.

It was SSgt. Brisslow's first tour in Vietnam. He readily acknowledged that and turned to me. "I'm not going to kid myself. It's your show, Henry. I'm willing to learn all I can from you."

"You're in charge, Sarge. But if I see you getting ready to screw up, I'll let you know," I replied.

We rested for a good thirty minutes before we resumed our patrols. Our orders were to head west for three hours, then reverse our direction. If all went well, we would regroup at our starting point, then make our way back to rejoin the rest of the battalion. I couldn't wait to get back and find out what the old man had been cooking up for the North Vietnamese.

Because of my experience, I wanted to walk point, but SSgt. Brisslow wanted me to stick close to him. He felt that if we got caught in a jam, he would need the combat experienced Marines with the main column. He was correct. There was little choice except to assign an inexperienced member of my squad to walk point.

"Listen closely, Terrel. Move really slowly. We aren't in any rush to get where we're going because we aren't going anywhere in particular. Trust your feelings. If you feel something isn't right, freeze on the spot, signal, and I'll come check it out. Look up and down before you step and then step softly."

I paused, reached into my pocket, pulled out a large marble and handed it to the slightly, nervous private.

"Hold on to my good luck charm," I continued as I patted him on his helmet.

"Okay, let's move out." Sgt. Brisslow ordered the rest of the men to stand by as Private Terrel moved out to take the point. He hesitated after going a few yards, and turned around. I winked as I gave him the a-okay sign by clinching my fist and sticking my thumb up. He returned my gesture and moved out. We had been humping through the jungle a good hour when I left my position at the front of the column and made my way back to the middle. I wanted to check with Sgt. Brisslow about replacing Terrel on point. I felt he had been out there long enough. SSgt. Brisslow agreed with me. But before I could relieve Terrel, the front of the column came to an abrupt halt.

"What's the hold up?" SSgt. Brisslow inquired. He signaled the rest of the column to halt.

"I'll check it out," I replied.

I hurried to the front of the column. When I reached it, I could see Terrel tugging away at something. The men at the front the column were all replacements and didn't know what to make of his movements. I was heading toward him to see what the problem was, when I realized, he had gotten tangled up in some vines. Just as I was about to holler at him to freeze and stop tugging, he pulled away and let out a sigh of relief. Much to my dismay, I saw the spoon of one of his grenades fly into the air. There was nothing I could do, except dive for cover.

"Hit the deck," I shouted, alerting the other members of the patrol.

Everyone dropped to the ground. A second later, the grenade went off, sending hundreds of pieces of shrapnel flying in a three hundred and sixty degree radius.

When the air cleared, I rushed to where Terrel had been standing seconds earlier. I knew what to expect. What I feared, had happened. When Terrel yanked himself free, he dislodged the safety pin in one of the grenades strapped to his chest. It wasn't a pretty sight. There wasn't much of him left. When the grenade exploded it set off the others he was carrying. The combined explosion had blown his body into dozens of bit pieces. SSgt. Brisslow made his way to where I was standing and looking at the fragments of what had been a man less than a minute ago.

"What happened?" he inquired. His eyes fell on the chunks of flesh scattered about. He quickly turned away, and threw his hand over his mouth in an attempt to suppress regurgitating. After a minute or so, he regained his composure long enough to repeat his original question.

"What happened?"

"He got tangled up in some vines. When he broke free, a vine must have wrapped around one of his grenades and pulled the pin. You're looking at the rest of the story," I answered rather coldly.

Although I didn't show it, I felt bad about what just happened. You always felt bad when someone bought it. I almost made the mistake of blaming myself for Terrel's death. If I hadn't left my position, I would have seen what he was doing in time to tell him to freeze, while I caught up with him and freed him from the vines. However, I quickly redirected my thoughts. "This is war and in war people die," I muttered.

The longer we stood around, the more likely we were to have unwanted visitors. I turned to SSgt. Brisslow. "If Charlie is anywhere in the neighborhood, he heard the explosion and he's probably going to pay us a visit real soon. There is nothing we can do for him. Let's see if we can find his tags and get out of here. We'd better catch up with the Lieutenant."

"I agree," SSgt. Brisslow responded. He then called for the radioman, who quickly joined us. "Get the Lieutenant on the horn," he bellowed.

While the sergeant was on the radio, I instructed several men to mount a quick search for Terrel's dog tags. One of them found the tags dangling from the branch of a nearby tree. I took them from him and gave them to SSgt. Brisslow.

Five minutes later, we were on our way to link up with the rest of the platoon. They were a good four miles east of us. Much to my surprise, we met with no enemy resistance. After we regrouped with the rest of the platoon and filled the Lieutenant in on what happened to Private Terrel, we learned that two men in the third squad had become victims of booby traps. Although they were both killed almost instantly, their bodies were still in one piece, and the Lieutenant was bringing them back with us.

We returned to the battalion bivouac area around dusk, without direct contact with the enemy or any more injuries. Neither the battalion commander nor Captain Jenkins seemed surprised to learn we had lost two men to booby traps. In fact, they expected us to have a much bigger problem than we did. They hadn't expected us to make direct contact with the enemy because they figured the North Vietnamese were busy preparing for their attack in the morning.

After the Colonel held a briefing for all the officers and staff noncommissioned officers, I learned what the CO was planning from Lieutenant Smith. The CO figured that if we remained where we were, we would have the advantage of knowing where the North Vietnamese soldiers would be in the morning. They would be where we were. He radioed our position to the rear and was assured that at least two squadrons of Phantoms would stand by to lend close air support in the morning. He was also assured that the artillery would be locked in on the coordinates surrounding our position. As soon as they received word, they would pound the hell out of the North Vietnamese. Elements of the Second Battalion-Ninth Marines would be standing by ready to drop behind the enemy, then presto, we would have them right where we wanted them: pinned down between two battalions of

Marines, with tons of artillery and rockets pouring in on their heads.

The night seemed to drag on forever. An hour or so before sunrise, the North Vietnamese Army started shelling us. We were dug in and waiting for the bombardment to begin. If enemy tactics held true to form, there would be a short lull between their rocket and artillery attack on our position before they came at us in human waves. If the CO's analysis of the situation was correct and his battle tactics worked, the entire battle would only last about an hour.

Still, I knew that before it was over there would be many dead Marines and enemy soldiers. I also knew that with the back door closed to them, the North Vietnamese, who had survived our surprise air and artillery attacks, would have nowhere to go except straight forward. That meant we would be engaged in some hand to hand combat. Shooting a man at a distance was one thing. Being close enough to touch him when you killed him was another.

There was little doubt in my mind concerning my ability to kill a man just as quickly face to face as I had at a distance, but I worried about the Marines in the battalion who were facing the enemy for the first time. Some of them would hesitate for a fraction of a second and that hesitation would cost them their lives.

We spent a good part of the night digging trenches and fox holes from which we would fight. At the same time the sun showed itself, the enemy began shelling our position. The word was passed to keep down and get ready. Our jets would streak overhead any minute now, delivering their deadly payload.

If the rest of the skipper's plan worked, before the North Vietnamese could recover fully from our surprise air attack, our artillery units would begin dropping shells on their positions. Along with our artillery attack, elements of the second battalion would land to their rear, supported by a large contingent of Huey and Cobra gunships. Cut off from a retreat route, the enemy would have no choice but to come at us. We would be ready and waiting for them.

Everything went like clockwork. Before the North Vietnamese Army could launch its planned surprise, we surprised them with our devastating close air support and the pinpoint accuracy of our artillery shells.

Driven prematurely from their concealed positions with nowhere to go but forward, a fanatical enemy charged our position. It was a suicidal effort. They had moved into position during the night and had planned to surprise us. Instead, they were caught with their pants down and were paying the price. The only way they could escape from our carefully executed trap would be to make their way to the jungle on the other side of us. We were well dug in and there was no way they could make it without suffering a large loss of personnel.

At least a thousand well-armed North Vietnamese regulars came at us determined to escape our trap and inflict as much harm on us as they could in the process. The fighting was fierce. Some North Vietnamese tried in vain to hold down the rear for their comrades, who were attempting to fight their way out of our trap.

The North Vietnamese soldiers fought gallantly. The ones who remained behind fought the advancing Second Battalion to the last man. A good part of the fighting was hand to hand combat, with an enemy determined to overrun our position. They had nothing to lose, and they fought like it. But in the end, we prevailed.

When the fighting was over, the area was littered with carnage, theirs and ours. We had won the battle, but at what price? When the final casualty figures were in, I learned that sixty-seven members of the Walking Dead had paid the ultimate price that a Marine must sometimes pay. Two dozen men of the second battalion were also killed in action. I stood looking at the rows of dead Marines and asking myself, "What was it all for?"

We were in the middle of nowhere. There was nothing around for miles except jungle and a few sparsely populated villages and hamlets. Our battalion had suffered the heaviest losses. Included among those killed in battle were SSgt. Brisslow and several members of my squad. A total of one hundred and eighty-two Marines were wounded in the battle. No one knew how many of them would eventually die as a result of their wounds. I had been hit in the face and hand by a couple of pieces of shrapnel, but the wounds weren't severe. I refused medical attention until the more seriously wounded were treated. Lieutenant Smith was shot up pretty bad and so were several NCOs in the battalion.

First, I saw to it that my wounded squad members were safely aboard med-evac choppers and on their way to an aid station or hospital, then I sought out a corpsman to tend to my wounds.

Meanwhile, some members of the second battalion were busy taking a body count. When I heard the final count, I wasn't at all surprised to learn that we had killed over five hundred North Vietnamese soldiers and captured one hundred and twenty-five. Although I grieved for my fallen comrades, I felt no anger toward the enemy. They were doing their job, just as we were doing ours. They had fought as gallantly as we had. While Doc was busy applying bandages to my facial wounds, several wounded prisoners of war were marched past me. I looked at Doc's blood-soaked hands and at the blood that flowed from the wounded prisoners. It all looked the same. After I was patched up, I refused immediate evacuation and returned to what was left of my platoon. We helped make a clearing in which we piled the enemy corpses atop one another, doused them with gasoline, then set the pile on fire.

Six hours later, we were back at Vandergrift Combat Base. I couldn't believe the festive atmosphere that engulfed the base. But within a few minutes, after learning why everyone was so happy, I joined in the festivities. It was like Christmas in July. While we were engaging the enemy in that fierce and costly battle, word had arrived at the base that our regiment would be part of the first troop withdrawal from Vietnam. President Nixon had begun his long-sought move toward "Peace with Honor."

Later that evening, I received even more good news. I would leave in the morning for Da Nang. First I would report to the hospital and have my wounds taken care of properly, then stay in Da Nang to assist with preparations for the departure of the Ninth Marines.

I wasted no time returning to my hooch and packing my gear. The memories of the fighting earlier in the day were still vividly dancing around in my head. I still grieved for all the men who had died in battle that day. As I looked at all the empty cots, a troubling thought entered my mind. Was there any 'Peace with Honor' for those brave souls who paid the ultimate price of war today?

Yet despite what I had experienced in battle that day, I was in "seventh heaven." Getting out of Vietnam alive and in the same physical condition that you arrived in, was the bottom line. After I packed my gear, I went and took a shower. When I returned to the hooch, I looked again at the empty cots. I stretched out on mine, closed my eyes and prayed, not for the men killed in battle because prayers couldn't help them now. Instead, I prayed for their families and their friends, both friend and foe. I asked the Lord to give them strength through the days ahead. I asked Him to help ease the pain of the wounded and help them to recover. Finally, I thanked Him for watching over me during my stay in hell and implored Him to not let anything freaky happen to me before I actually was out of there.

After I finished praying, I lay awake for a long time, thinking of what I had seen and experienced in Vietnam. I still didn't know why we were involved in this rotten war. But I did know it would leave its mark on me. My last thoughts before drifting to sleep were of Miriko, Tom, the other children and Chevalier. The two days that I had spent with them had been a couple of the happiest of my young life, so far. I looked forward to seeing them again.

CHAPTER FOURTEEN

The wind gently stroked my face as I stood gazing over the side of the ship, staring blankly at the blackened night. Clouds filled the sky, blocking all light from the heavens. Two weeks had passed since I left Vandergrift Combat Base. The two days I had spent so far aboard the USS Paul Revere seemed to drag on and on. I wouldn't be heading home just yet, but I was safely out of Vietnam. Our unit would be stationed in Okinawa, and I would remain with them until my full year of overseas duty had expired. My stay in Da Nang, while assisting in the preparations for our withdrawal from Vietnam, didn't turn out as I had hoped it would. The pain and the sorrow of the war didn't end for me that last day at Vandergrift Combat Base. When I arrived in Da Nang, after I had myself checked out at the hospital, I reported to Marine Corps Headquarters, Da Nang. I was assigned to a company that was being set up to facilitate the withdrawal of the first 25,000 Marines from Vietnam. After settling in, I requested and was granted a few days of liberty.

Immediately afterward I left the base, hailed a cab and instructed the driver to take me to Chevalier's house. I could hardly wait to see the children again, especially Miriko. My heart pumped vigorously as the cab neared the familiar sight of the long stone wall that surrounded Chevalier's home. I paid the driver and dashed through the gate leading to the house, only to stop dead in my tracks. Where a house had stood just a few weeks ago, there was nothing but a bombed-out shell.

"No!" I cried aloud.

I ran frantically toward what was left of the house. "Chevalier! Miriko!" I shouted.

Without stopping, I ran through the rubble into the house and courtyard. Both were empty. The only signs of the children that remained were empty swings swaying in the breeze and several charred cribs under the trees, where the infants used to nap. I was crushed. I fell on my knees and buried my head in my hands. "Why?" I cried aloud, thinking the worst.

It took me a while to regain my composure. When I finally did, I went back into the bombed out remains of the house. My imagination began to get the best of me. I could hear the children laughing.I could feel their smiles. Slowly, I made my way to the bedroom where Miriko used to sleep. Virtually the entire room had been reduced to rubble. The only part still standing was the wall containing the painting of the American and Republic of Vietnam flags. In an uncontrollable fit of frustration and anger, I pulled out my forty- five and emptied the entire clip of rounds into the picture. After holstering my pistol, I walked over to the spot where just a few weeks earlier I had gently tucked Miriko in bed. All that remained of her bed was a pile of burnt wood on the floor.

For some strange reason, I felt driven to sift through the debris. The pile of burnt wood felt cold to my touch. Suddenly, I touched a piece of metal. I lifted it from the mess and clutched my discovery in both hands. What I found was the music box I had given Miriko. The wooden replica of a phonograph that had housed it had burned away. I flopped onto the floor and began to rub the soot off the metal casing. The crank was also made of metal and when I finished cleaning the music box, I started turning the crank. To my surprise, it turned with ease, and when it was fully wound, I released the crank. The sound of Greensleeves rolled off. I lost count of how long I sat there listening to it. It was dark when I finally left the room and headed back to Da Nang.

I spent the entire evening and well into the night desperately trying to find out what had happened to Chevalier and the children. All that I was able to learn was that the house had been hit a week earlier when a Air Force jet fighter crashed into it. It pained me to learn that Chevalier and several of the children were killed in the crash. During the remainder of my stay in Da Nang, I spent every free moment trying to locate the survivors of Chevalier's family. All my efforts were in vain. They seemed to have vanished into thin air. Although I told myself I was searching for all the surviving children, deep down inside I knew that more than anything else, I wanted to know that Miriko had survived. I desperately wanted to see her again. I promised myself that if she were okay, I would find a way to get her to America.

The sounds of the ocean pounding against the side of the ship snapped me out of my painful remembrances. I reached in my pocket, pulled out the music box and slowly turned the crank. I listened to the tune again in an attempt to comfort myself. Silently, I prayed that Miriko had survived the crash, was safe in another home, and that life would somehow be kind to her. When the music box wound down, my thoughts drifted back to my last few days in Vietnam. The day before I boarded the USS Paul Revere for the journey to Okinawa, I received my first letter from Bass. He was in San Diego awaiting his discharge. The same day, I had learned from Captain Jenkins that Lieutenant Smith was in a Naval hospital in Japan. He was expected to recover fully from his battle wounds. The good news brightened up my day.

The day we were leaving Vietnam, there was a big parade in our honor, staged in Da Nang. Thousands of Vietnamese lined the streets leading to the docks, waving American and Republic of Vietnam flags and shouting "God bless America."

As a member of the advance party, I was already waiting at the docks for the rest of the regiment to arrive and board the ships. Thank God for small favors, was just one of my thoughts as I watched the men of my battalion marching down the street in full combat gear.

A huge grandstand had been erected at the end of the dock. At the front was a podium bearing the seal of the President of the Republic of South Vietnam. Behind, were rows of seats, filled with top military brass and South Vietnamese officials. "We'll never get out of here. By the look of things, we're in for a couple of hours of bullshit speeches," I commented to a sailor standing next to me. My observations were correct. I felt sorry for my comrades who were forced to stand in formation, in full battle dress, for a good two hours, while the blistering sun beat down on them. Although several of them collapsed, it didn't stop the charade taking place atop the platform.

Official after official and general after general made one speech after another. The stricken Marines were simply picked up and taken to sick bay aboard one of the ships, while the rest of the troops closed ranks. I sat in the shade of a jeep and felt bad about the rest of my regiment, having to endure all the bullshit formalities. But I didn't feel bad enough to go over and join them.

The President of the Republic of Viet-Nam, Nguyen Van Thieu, made the last speech. He opened it by lavishing us with praise.

"I extend my most heartfelt thanks and sincere congratulations for the incomparable feats-of-arms displayed by the regiment during nearly four years in Vietnam."

He ended his speech with the following words.

"To the families of the fallen heroes and to the wounded troops, I should like to ask you to extend my most heartfelt sense of gratitude for their incomparable contribution to the cause of Peace and Liberty in Vietnam."

When he was finished, everyone seated in the grandstand stood up for the playing of the national anthems of both countries.

"Finally!" I remarked.

The order was given for the troops to begin boarding the ships. I was about to start up the jeep and drive it over to the LST that it was going to be shipped out on, when I noticed a woman standing near the edge of the crowd gathered on the docks. She handed something to a little girl and pointed to a group of Marines standing near a truck. At first, I didn't pay any attention to her actions. I assumed she had given the child a gift to bestow upon the departing Marines.

Suddenly I noticed the same woman turn and begin to hurriedly make her way through the crowd, away from the dock. Immediately, my suspicions were aroused. I jumped out of the jeep and began running toward the little girl to get a look at what she was carrying. She was around thirty feet from the group of Marines near the truck, when I got close enough to see what she was clutching in her small hands; a grenade!

My immediate response was to run over, grab her and snatch the grenade from her before she could open her hands and release the handle. Once the handle was released, the armed grenade would explode in approximately three seconds. Before I could reach her, she stopped less than twenty feet from the Marines. They were strangers to her, and she wasn't going to get any closer to them. I froze for a second when I saw her extend her arms and release her grip on the grenade. At the same time, she gestured for the Marines to come and get the present she had been sent to give them. One of the Marines started to step toward her, when the handle of the grenade sprung free. He realized immediately what the child was carrying and shouted, "Live grenade!" as he dove for cover.

Meanwhile, I had unholstered my forty-five and chambered a round. The other Marines immediately hit the deck and scrambled for cover. I took careful aim at the girl holding the live grenade with a bewildered look on her face. She was, no doubt, confused by the actions of the Marines, to whom she was offering what she believed to be a present.

The three seconds that had lapsed between the time the grenade had been armed and when I pulled the trigger of my pistol seemed like an eternity. One round was all that was needed. The bullet struck her in the temple and ripped off the top of her head as it passed through. Blood gushed from her head, like red, hot, molten lava from an erupting volcano. The grenade fell to the ground and the little girl's now lifeless body slumped on top of it. I dropped to the ground and covered my head with my arms. A fraction of a second later, the grenade exploded, ripping through her body. Pieces of flesh and shrapnel went flying in every direction.

Seconds after the explosion, I stood up and stared at the spot where the little girl had been. "You had no choice," I told myself aloud as I fought back the tears. I really didn't. I remember my exact thoughts as I pulled the trigger. It's too late to stop her and, if I don't kill her, the grenade sure as hell will. She might not die instantly, but there's no way she's going to survive the blast.

Children are always the most innocent victims of war. The girl I had just killed was only doing what she was told. Most likely, the woman simply instructed her to hold onto the grenade tightly and go give it to the nice GIs. The innocent child had no idea what it was she was carrying. I remember thinking of my little sister back home. She was around the same age, as the little girl appeared to be. Suddenly I got sick to my stomach and began throwing up.

There was a lot of commotion on the docks, because of the explosion. It took a few minutes for things to settle back down. Several intended victims of the dead child's "gift" ran over to me, and began congratulating me on my heroic action. I couldn't believe them. They thought I shot her to save their lives. Perhaps subconsciously I had. But consciously I was only thinking of the little girl being torn apart by the exploding grenade. In a few days, they would most likely forget the entire incident. But I knew I would have to live with the memory of my decision for the rest of my life.

The sound of trash dumped overboard brought me back to the present. While I had been reliving the events of the past few days in my mind, the thick cloud cover had broken up and the full moon, surrounded by hundreds of stars, was now visible, shining brightly and reflecting off the ocean. I slowly tilted my head back and looked at the night sky. I stood gazing wide-eyed at the moon. A description of the moon that I had once read in an astrology book resurfaced in my mind.

In the book, the moon was described as the "Mother of the Earth." It went on to say, "As does any loving mother, it watched tirelessly over her beloved only child." Slowly rotating my head, I continued to scan the sky. I was sure of one thing, someone had been watching over me.

It was starting to get a little chilly as the night air embraced me, so I headed below to my sleeping quarters. Right before I stepped through the hatch, I took another look at the sky and thought, in a few hours, the sun will once again create the illusion that it is rising in the sky, signaling the start of a new day. A new day for the world and a new day for me. Starting tomorrow, I will begin trying to put the memories of my time in Vietnam behind me.

THE END

THE AUTHOR - 1969
1 WEEK BEFORE REPORTING TO VIETNAM

THE AUTHOR - 1969
ONE MONTH AFTER ARRIVAL IN VIETNAM
VANDERGRIFT COMBAT BASE - QUANG TRI PROVINCE

AUTHOR AT VANDEGRIFT COMBAT BASE
VIETNAM 1969

Marines of the 1st Battalion, 9th Marines, form up at the docks in Da Nang for a convoy-marking their departure from Vietnam after months of combat operations, 1969. They are about to board the USS *Paul Revere* for Okinawa, Japan.

RICHARD HENRY

Richard Henry was born, raised and educated in New York City. After his service in the United States Marine Corps, which included a tour in Viet Nam, he returned to New York where he worked as a teacher and coordinator of Alternative High Schools.

In 1983, he moved to Oklahoma to serve as the Director of Alternative Dispute Resolution for four counties under the direction of the Oklahoma State Supreme Court.

In 1990, he moved to California and set up a training program for formally incarcerated youth. In 1992, he served as the "Economic and Business Development Coordinator" for military base closures.

He published his first book of poetry, "Beyond the Skull" in 1976. His novel, "Of Days Gone By" was first published in 1990, followed by his second novel, "Short Timer" in 2002. His third book, "The Extraordinary Life of an Extraordinary Bear" was published in 2022.

www.ingramcontent.com/pod-product-compliance
Lightning Source LLC
Chambersburg PA
CBHW060509130626
46553CB00002B/438